THE CAUSE TO LIVE FOR

THE CAUSE TO LIVE FOR
Building a legacy bigger than you

Vineyard Churches UK & Ireland

First published in Great Britain in 2018

Vineyard Books (UK & Ireland)
an imprint of
Society for Promoting Christian Knowledge
36 Causton Street
London SW1P 4ST
www.spck.org.uk

British Library Cataloguing-in-Publication Data
A catalogue record for this book is available from the British Library

ISBN 978–1–9164566–0–0
eBook ISBN 978–1–9164566–1–7

Typeset by Fakenham Prepress Solutions, Fakenham, Norfolk NR21 8NL
First printed in Great Britain by Jellyfish Print Solutions
Subsequently digitally printed in Great Britain

eBook by Manila Typesetting Company

Produced on paper from sustainable forests

Contents

About Vineyard Churches UK & Ireland

The **Vineyard movement** is built on God's transforming word and is made up of people who worship God with passion, intimacy and expectation.

We are a growing movement with over 2,500 churches worldwide, with more than 140 (at the time of writing) in the UK and Ireland alone.

We exist to serve people, especially the poor and the vulnerable, and we communicate the goodness of Jesus with compassion and generosity.

We are God's children, extending his Kingdom together everywhere in every way.

We will make disciples, develop leaders, plant churches and contribute to the blessing of the whole Body of Christ.

The **Cause to Live For** is a collective of young adults from Vineyard churches in the UK and Ireland who are desperate to see a move of God's Kingdom breaking out across our nations.

Find your nearest Vineyard church at
<www.vineyardchurches.org.uk>.

THE CAUSE TO LIVE FOR

Foreword

Causes.

Everyone has some sort of cause that they live for. For some people their career becomes their cause; some might see earning money as their purpose, while for others an environmental issue or a focus on family is what keeps them going.

As people who have encountered the living God, we think differently. We believe that each person is placed on this earth to glorify God and to work in partnership with him in extending his Kingdom.

We are all on a journey of discovering the next thing that God has for us. We look to see what the Father is doing and cooperate with him in that. He has plans for us, and he wants us to join him on an adventure of his design.

Wherever you are on your journey, we want you to know that he is good, he loves you and he wants to know you intimately.

Our prayer for you is that you will be caught up by Christ, his Church and his cause, as he reveals his unique design for your life, and that this book will be a helpful tool in this process.

John and Debby Wright
National Directors
Vineyard Churches UK & Ireland

A FEW 'I WANTS'.
A LIFE OF 'I WILLS'.
A LIFE OF LEGACY.

Be a history maker

Andy Smith

Andy leads Belfast City Vineyard and, together with his wife Harmony, also provides leadership for the Vineyard churches in Ireland.

You are a precious demographic. When we release young leaders, amazing things happen for the Kingdom. The Vineyard is passionate about releasing you, not holding you back. I'm honoured – if not a little surprised – to be invited to share some thoughts with you. You see, I'm forty-something going on sixty-something; I'm a pretty radical introvert, so when I was asked to offer some thoughts to a group of people in their twenties and thirties, I couldn't for the life of me work out what I would say. Thankfully, I figured it out.

It goes something like this. I live in Belfast. Our offices and ministry centres are right in the city centre. I was on the bus, early one morning, heading in and praying to the Lord, 'I really need to figure out what you want to say to these guys.' As I was travelling, I thought I would see who else had been asked to contribute. I saw that a guy called Martin Smith had. My mind instantly flitted back to a time in my late teens, early twenties, when Martin's band Delirious? had recently released a song called 'History Maker'. The lyrics proclaim that each of us is a history maker, a speaker of truth to all humanity, and that we shall stand. This became almost like a soundtrack to a really potent time in my life. It was one of the first times I heard that it was OK to reach for more in worship.

I grew up in a pretty traditional context, and there's nothing wrong with that. But when I heard 'History Maker' it was one of the first times I'd ever articulated an 'I want' to God. I never knew you could want to do anything for Jesus. That he might want something for me, other than to be good. I didn't know that we could dream with him, reach for things, that he might put some wants in our hearts. Things that we give ourselves to, things that we sacrifice for, to see his change and transformation come to things and people we care deeply about. Walking through Belfast, a few tears coming down my cheeks, I knew I wanted to talk about a few 'I wants' surrounded by a lifetime of 'I wills'. About building a Kingdom legacy in your life that will overflow far beyond you and enable others around you to access life in Jesus and his gracious Kingdom. A few 'I wants', a life of 'I wills' and a life of legacy.

What on earth do I mean by having a lifetime of 'I wills'? Well, if an 'I want' is like a calling or dream, something that grabs the heart, that we know we must be a part of, an action or mission or assignment that we are given for a season, then an 'I will' is the other side of that coin. An 'I will' is a response to who Jesus is. It's not a reaching out for something; it's a response to something. It's the life we build around him. It's the rhythms we cultivate to stay close to him. Because I have encountered Jesus, *I will* build my life around him, in response to all that he has done for me.

In Matthew 13.44, Jesus tells us: 'The kingdom of heaven is like treasure hidden in a field. When a man found it, he hid it again, and then in his joy went and sold all he had and bought that field.' So he tells this story about the Kingdom of God, life in God's Kingdom and the opportunity for us. An 'I will' is like this man who finds treasure and joyfully sells everything he has to buy the field. It's a *response* to discovering the Kingdom. It's a response that says it's worth everything – all I have, everything I have.

How should we respond to the Jesus who loves us with an everlasting love, who is Saviour and Lord, who went to the cross for us, who is at the right hand of the Father, who is available to us right now and in the hour of our need? The only response is to offer our whole lives to buy the field with great joy. When we encounter the Kingdom, when we encounter Jesus and our chance of life with him, we respond. We say 'I will . . . I will respond to you.'

Our 'I wills' are our response to his glory, his goodness, his mercy and the possibility of living in the Kingdom. Jesus actually tells us where to start. He tells us the first and greatest 'I will' response in John 15. Here he explains that the appropriate response is what he invites us into: a life of friendship and abiding with him. He says to his disciples, and he says to us:

I am the true vine, and my Father is the gardener. He cuts off every branch in me that bears no fruit, while every branch that does bear fruit he prunes so that it will be even more fruitful. You are already clean because of the word I have spoken to you. Remain in me, as I also remain in you. No branch can bear fruit by itself; it must remain in the vine. Neither can you bear fruit unless you remain in me.

I am the vine; you are the branches. If you remain in me and I in you, you will bear much fruit; apart from me you can do nothing.

(John 15.1–5)

He's inviting us to abide, dwell, live or remain in him, as he promises to remain in us. He uses the image of a vine with branches bearing fruit. It's not about struggle and striving, or about trying to please God. It's not wondering if you're making the grade. It's not a distant thing. It's close and deep friendship with Jesus: friendship with him as our first goal and response.

Our greatest 'I will' in response to him is to cultivate rhythms of love and dependency, where you actually know him and receive his resources and presence and power, as we live out this eternal Kingdom life. In the Gospels, Jesus keeps telling us he is available in and through belief, trust and faith in him. We're to know him and abide in him. Before we do anything else, before we produce, we remain. We pursue a life of peace and rest in his loving presence. Out of that place we bear fruit. You were made for relationship with him. You were made to give yourself as a response. You were made to give yourself to a life of deep, transforming and empowering friendship with him. Will that be your first and greatest 'I will' as a response to Jesus?

This is what I try to do. I try to live out what Jesus invites us into in John 15. To pursue Jesus and friendship with him, then let what he has done in me impact and overflow into the world around me. All the 'I wants', all the things we want to reach for and the impact that we dream about, are wonderful – but Jesus tells us that they are all unsustainable, apart from friendship with him.

Here are a few more important 'I wills' in response to Jesus for me – and I hope they are for you. The next one is worship. In response to Jesus, *I will* cultivate a life of worship. Not worship when I feel like it, not worship when there's a smoke machine and an incredible worship team. I will cultivate a life of worship wherever I happen to be. You're probably thinking that all life can be worship and I, of course, agree and endorse that. But what I am referring to here are dedicated times of worship, when we open our mouths to worship by ourselves, corporately, in a small group or in children's ministry, or wherever we happen to be.

Do we build a life of worship? An intimate tending to the presence of Jesus? A life of adoration that leads to an encounter with him? That's our inheritance as a movement. Worship that isn't just singing songs about Jesus – but rather singing to him, because he is worthy and he deserves everything we have to give and more. When we encounter him in his presence by his Spirit, he visits us as we pour out our hearts in worship and praise to him.

Worship has been, and still continues to be, a special place. A 'thin' place, where the space between heaven and earth is far narrower than usual. We offer Jesus all that we are and he visits us. He breathes on us as people, he heals us, he encourages us, he empowers us. In response to who Jesus is, will we build lives of worship?

Going back to 'History Maker' and that time in my life – it was in worship that Jesus invited me to more. It was in worship that he changed me. There was lots more to it but it was worship that gave me language for what was going on in my heart – that I could then pour back out to him. That's so important. Have one of your responses, one of your big 'I wills' be to cultivate and build a life of worship. Jesus deserves it all and you were made for the encounters that come through a life of worship.

Another 'I will' is serving. In response to who Jesus is, *I will* serve. *I will* become a servant for he became a servant to me. Because I know him, I'm resting in him, I am secure enough in my identity as a follower and friend of Jesus that I don't have to be the centre of the story. I can make him the hero of the story. I will serve Jesus. I can serve and love others in profound ways because I know I'm loved with an everlasting love. I know I'm safe and secure in the Kingdom of God, who loves me very, very much, in the presence of his son Jesus.

Will you make serving and service one of your 'I wills'? Will you serve in your family? Will you serve in your relationships? Will you serve in your city, in your workplace, in your universities, in your schools? Wherever you are, will you model out the life and security that is found in Jesus by making serving one of your 'I wills'? I know many of you are already doing this, but if you're not, I want to encourage you to commit to serve in a new way. Will you honour what Jesus is doing in your church, even if you're frustrated with some of the things other people are doing there? Will you do more than just join a rota? Will you start something, lead something, bear weight? Bring life and love and mercy? Will you be dependable because you've met Jesus and you have made serving, and serving his bride the Church, whom he loves, a non-negotiable 'I will'?

Another 'I will' is prayer and life in the Scriptures. Will you build a life of prayer? Will you build a life of attention to his Word, as a response to him? Will you allow his Word and time in prayer to form you? The most powerful and compelling people I know, know where their Bible is, and they know how to pray. They're students of the Scriptures. They know them. They have them memorised. But more than that, their lives are shaped and moulded by the Scriptures. They listen to them. They know how to gain wisdom there. They meet the Lord in the Scriptures and in prayer, and they're able to give that away to other people. They allow the truths of the Scriptures to lead them to life and hope and identity and relationship with Jesus. And obedience to Jesus. Will you make that one of your 'I wills'?

Very closely related to this are solitude and silence: will you make this one of your responses to Jesus? There is so much noise out there. There is so much distraction – from social media through to the way we do friendships these days and get information. It's all so intense and present all the time and it drowns out so much of what God is trying to say. If you want to make an impact, will you commit, as a response to Jesus, to intentional times of solitude and silence? Where you decide to get away from the noise and allow him to speak to you, allow him to love you, in a place where you listen to him? The most important part of my day as an 'I will' response is the time that I set aside to sit in silence before him, loving him, allowing him to love me, listening to him, as I'm attentive to his presence. Would you think about that as an 'I will' response to Jesus? Will you set up some boundaries for that?

Another 'I will' is holiness and purity. In response to Jesus, *I will* live a life of holiness and purity, especially sexual purity. Will you make that an 'I will'? Will we get serious about obeying Jesus, listening to him for words of life and putting it into practice in our real lives, no matter what that may seem to cost us? Will we get serious about loving what he loves and avoiding what he says destroys and enslaves us, hurting others and keeping us from his loving presence? Will we put boundaries around what we watch, what we do, how we interact with other people? Will we put boundaries around our speech, and boundaries about what we tell ourselves and the narratives we allow to form inside us and shape us? Will we learn to have a 'whatever it takes' attitude to reach for purity in an age where we are bombarded with ways to sin and dehumanise others and ourselves?

There are so many more 'I wills' we could look at. We need everyone not only to talk about life in Jesus but also to live *out* life with Jesus. To be disciples and invite others to become disciples, to be part of the work of Jesus and the Kingdom as he remakes this world, one life at a time. Believe it or not, your 'I wills', your responses to Jesus, your willingness to live out a life of friendship with him, matter profoundly to him, because your 'I wills' sustain the 'I wants'.

The thing is, your 'I wills' are hidden. It's your secret life with Jesus. But they sustain the big 'I wants' – the dreams, the callings, the impact that Jesus has for you in the world – the fruitfulness that he spoke of in John 15. If we just live in the realm of dream and impact and all the stuff we're going to do, and we don't spend any time living from the place of friendship, peace and rest in the presence of Jesus, it will be a body without a skeleton, or lungs without the breath of God upon them. We will not have a life of friendship with Jesus, we will not taste fruit that will last, and we will approach him like a slave, instead of a friend.

Are we living the kind of life with God that will sustain what he's calling us to? For a long time, I didn't understand why we couldn't just focus on the calling of God on us, and all the dreams about the world being impacted and changed – all the 'I wants' – and expect it to go well. The life you build with Jesus – the secret life, the 'I wills' – will sustain and support the fruitful life. We can't just think about the things we want to do, or the 'wants' we're called to, without developing the rhythms or the attitude and the secret life with Jesus that's required to get us there and sustain us there. For a long time, I knew I was called to a lot. I didn't plan to have rhythms in place that were specifically designed to sustain what he was calling me to do. Do you? Do you have a life of 'I wills' that will sustain a few 'I wants'?

Well, let's talk about our 'I wants'. I have a few 'I wants'. Just as, in John 15, he tells us that fruitfulness without friendship with

Jesus doesn't work, it's also clear from the same passage that a life of abiding without fruitfulness doesn't work. You have to have both. It's just that abiding comes first. So, we get to have some 'I wants' sustained by a lot of 'I wills'. We get to have active, risk-taking engagement with the world, that place where we contend for something. Where we look at the world and say 'I need to do something about that'; or 'I want to see an end to that'; or 'I want more of that and it's worth it.' Where, empowered by the Spirit, we visualise a dream or a hope or a desire – then see it come to fruition or spend ourselves trying. Because I've built my life around Jesus, he has invited me to be with him on mission. To get out of the boat and be part of what he is doing in the world. We get to have some 'I wants'.

What are your 'I wants'? For some people, it's planting a church. For others, it's to break cycles of poverty and brokenness. For others, it's to start a business that impacts the city with the Kingdom. For some, it's to revolutionise healthcare. For others, it's to revolutionise an aspect of education. To break the chains of injustice. To enter into politics in a Kingdom way. What are your 'I wants'? Keep them in mind, because your 'I wants' are going to require a few things of you.

First, they're going to require you to experience heartbreak. When God plants dreams in your heart, he's going to allow you to see and experience why you should care. That means heartbreak. You can read in your Bible about Nehemiah the wall-builder. When he hears about the destruction of Jerusalem, his first action is weeping and heartbreak, then it's prayer and then he does something about it and takes action.

So, are you up for this? Allowing Jesus to show you the hurt and the pain and the brokenness – and then to show you his solutions and your part in them. The Cause to Live For has been blessed to receive teaching from the co-founder and Chief Executive of the anti-slavery and anti-trafficking organisation Hope for Justice. Now, their 'I want' – to live in a world free from slavery – is undoubtedly an amazing want, but I bet you Ben Cooley and the incredible people who work there have seen the pain, heartbreak and sorrow that make up the 'why' behind their want.

For me personally, when I visited Belfast on a ministry trip, I was heartbroken. I knew I had to be a part of what Jesus was doing in that great city. If you talk to anyone who has taken a risk or said 'I want', you can bet something has caught their heart; that it's personal; that they can't walk away because they've seen the heartbreak and they know they need to do something about it. What's personal to you? What – in your university, town, city, family, church, around the world – is breaking your heart? What if heartbreak is actually a call to action? Your 'I wants' will need you to experience heartbreak. They'll require action and perseverance. Anybody can talk but not many people act to change situations that break their hearts. I want to encourage you to do real things, for the real world, that involve God and the real Kingdom. Facebook outrage is not real action; it won't get you very far.

Do you remember that horrific and heartbreaking photograph of the refugee boy who drowned and was washed up on the beach? Do you remember how that stirred the world? Well, right around then, just as in many churches, there was a lot of noise in our church about how we needed to gather a collection; we needed to send some money to fix it. We as a leadership team prayed about it and encouraged people to give money directly to the organis-ations already doing a wonderful job to address this need. But we as a church have a compassion ministry. The leadership team suggested that every week we should keep preaching the gospel, giving food to, befriending and loving asylum seekers and refugees – from the very countries our church was now talking about – in our city. That we should start doing more of this ministry. Not many people wanted to do that. Talking about it is easier than doing it. 'I wants' are wonderful. But they require action and perseverance. And it's going to cost you. It's going to require you to say no sometimes to good things so you can say yes robustly and wholeheartedly to what Jesus is placing before you.

It doesn't only require action, it requires courage. It's amazing to me just how many Scriptures there are that speak against fear, that invite us into courage. We need courage because the things before us look – or are – impossible, or involve risk, risk of failure, risk of being misunderstood. We also need courage because we meet resistance from the enemy, from people, from the world we live in and its trajectory. There's something about the Kingdom of God where we have to be up for some fighting. For so many people, the 'I wants' in your life mean occupying some new ground, pioneering some new things, doing things that haven't been done yet, or haven't been done in a long time. You're going to have to fight for that ground. That's going to take courage.

We don't grow when we're comfortable. Growth comes when we have to contend for things and fight for things. We have to understand that Jesus inaugurates or welcomes in the Kingdom of God, and he wins ultimate victory for us on the cross. But his Church, empowered by the Spirit, awaits the full consummation of that victory when he returns. In the meantime, we continue to advance against the kingdom of the enemy, occupying ground, taking back ground – through healing, through deliverance, through salvation, through breaking the chains of injustice. We're to take some ground and that requires courage.

There are some things you can only learn about faith, only learn about Jesus, by contending for something – in you, in your city, in your family, in your church, or wherever you happen to be. Unfortunately, the only way that I know of building courage is by being courageous – even when you don't feel like it. In other words, being afraid, but doing it anyway.

I'm not originally from Belfast. In 2001, my wife Harmony and I moved from the USA to be interns, which we did for a year and then . . . surprise! We were appointed leaders of the church. And we haven't left yet. The night before we left, we were staying with my parents. I was in my old bedroom alone, doing some last bits of packing, and I began to realise the risk. We didn't really know anybody in this church – or even in Belfast. I began to be terrified, I began shaking. If I'd had to get on the plane at that moment, I couldn't have done it. That's how frightened I was. I prayed for a long time. You know what got me on the plane? I knew, somewhere in my heart, that I would regret it for the rest of my life if I didn't. Even if I went and it was a complete failure, at least I wouldn't have to live with regret.

Your 'I wants' will probably be terrifying at times. And that's OK. We build courage until we face our fear and do what we're made for. What we're called to, anyway. Take courage – you have a Church of people behind you that values risk-taking for the Kingdom.

So, what are your unique 'I wants'? What are the things that you're willing to act on, to persevere and take risks for, and to show radical courage for? I pray that the Spirit of God gives you clarity and hope and peace and joy – and that some amazing things begin in his presence.

I want to close by talking about legacy. Having lots of 'I wills', a few 'I wants' and a huge amount of faith in our God builds legacy. What do I mean by legacy? Legacies are things handed down from one generation to the next – or from one person or group to another. It could be an amount of money, or property, or a way of thinking about culture. It could be values. It could be worldview or character. It could be anything. Something that someone contends for and stewards in such a way that momentum is built and passed down to other people – so that they can access something more easily than the founder was able to do. That's what legacies and inheritances do – they overflow beyond the founder or original person and they allow those that come after them to walk easily in something that the founder had to fight for.

Lots of 'I wills' and a few 'I wants' over time will build a Kingdom legacy that will overflow beyond you and influence many others – for Jesus' sake and his glory. You know you're hitting legacy questions when you begin to ask, 'What will I do with what

I have been given? Is it just for me and my comfort? Is it just so I can have a great life and be noticed?' I want you to have a great life, an amazing life. But that's only going to happen when we begin to ask, 'Could what I have go beyond me and release others into blessing?'

So, would you steward the life you have been given to aim for a legacy? Will you steward all your life and all your relationships, your gifts, your skills? Will you remember that you have access to King Jesus and all the resources you need? Will you take all you have and all you will have and use it to bring maximum benefit to all those around you, to those who will come after you, even those who you don't know and will never meet? Will you let Jesus build in and through you and cause it to overflow? You begin to think differently about life when you contend for legacy. Do the choices you're making right now prioritise the legacy Jesus wants to build through your life? Do the choices you're making today reflect the 'I wills' and 'I wants' that are around your life right now? What decisions, what responses, do you need to make today? Which battles do you need to fight today so that your children and your grandchildren and many, many others can stand upon and access the legacy that God builds, so that they can do greater things in God's Kingdom than we could ever do – and have access to more?

First, we respond by having lots of 'I wills'. Then have a few specific 'I wants' that you're reaching for. Then steward them all for a Kingdom legacy that extends far beyond you. It will be the hardest thing you ever do. But it will be the best thing that you ever do.

ALL THE JOURNEYS OF FAITH BEGIN WITH A DREAM, SOMETHING GOD PLACES IN OUR HEARTS.

Transform nations

Jen Rankine

Jen planted Cardiff Vineyard Church with her husband, James, and together they are part of the Vineyard Churches UK & Ireland Leadership Group with responsibility for church planting.

I wanted to start by telling you about a tender moment I had with one of my daughters. I have three little girls: aged six, four and two. Because I have three children, it's actually hard to get that one-to-one time with each of them, so when those little moments come along, it's really precious. I remember when my middle daughter, Isobel, crept downstairs one evening and peered into the room. She curled up on my lap and looked up at me with a look that said, 'This is a Mummy moment, just me and Mummy.' I stroked her hair, cherishing this moment in my heart. She lifted her hand to my face and started to stroke it in return. Oh, so precious! Then she said, 'Mummy, you've got lines.' I realised then, not for the first time, that I was truly on the path to becoming wizened!

Now, the reason I'm telling you this story is because I turned thirty-seven this year. My husband turned to me one evening and said, 'Darling, you're nearly out of the Cause to Live For age bracket. It's about time you spoke at a conference!' Talk about flattering someone into taking on a task!

I was asked a couple of months ago: 'What is your vision for the Cause to Live For generation?'

Something started to rise up as if Jesus had planted the answer in my heart and it was waiting for this question to be asked. I replied, 'What I see is a generation of young adults terrified to take risks, fearful of stepping aside from the path of everyone else, fearful of getting it wrong, fearful of possibility and expectation; we don't care because we don't dare. Indecision, apathy and fear are paralysing us – and I can't bear it.'

I work as a GP in inner-city Cardiff. As I go to work each day, I see brokenness around me. Broken families, child sex abuse, severe mental illness, poverty and hopelessness – so often it overwhelms me. Sometimes when a patient leaves the room, I want to shut the door and cry. The problems of this society feel too big, don't they? And that's only a small group of people, in a small city, on a small island – never mind the rest of the world.

Do you know what else I think? We need more churches. We need more people in churches being the Church. We need more people standing up, more Christians shaping our society, addressing our attitudes, and changing and challenging our distorted views about Jesus, people and society – because we have got it wrong. We need people who have actually got the guts to stand up and speak up and then change things.

So, I want to look at this fear but also I want to look at faith. I want you to be encouraged that you're not alone. That we can stand up and step out in faith. Fear can be OK, it's how we respond to it that matters. It is my prayer that God speaks to you and God stirs you. That he reminds you that whatever he is calling you to, he's with you and he believes in you.

I want to start by looking at the Vineyard movement. You see, this movement in the UK and Ireland is at a crossroads – a point at which to take a breath and step into a new season. This movement was started by John and Ele Mumford, who left everything they had to plant a Vineyard church in London, years ago, that would grow into the movement in the UK and Ireland that we see today. The leadership of the movement has been taken over by John and Debby Wright, who equally sacrificed to join the Mumfords, first in London and now in Trent Vineyard, Nottingham. But it wasn't only them. It wasn't just the Mumfords and the Wrights. The Vineyard in the UK and Ireland only came to life because many, many others took faith decisions to risk, to sweat, to sacrifice, to trust in what they could not see.

Jeremy and Elaine Cook, who lead Hull Vineyard, have a really amazing story. Jeremy came to faith as a young adult after university. He and Elaine were married. He was an extremely successful businessman who had risen up through the ranks of EMI. At the time, it was one of the top three record companies in the world. His title was European Executive Vice-President and Chief Financial Officer. You can imagine the salary that went with that title!

At the time, Jeremy and Elaine were living in London. Out of nowhere, God spoke to them about moving back to Hull, where he was originally from, and planting a church there. Responding to the call, he gave up this illustrious job and they moved to Beverley – a lovely, leafy suburb outside Hull – and planted an independent church. These were his words: 'But the Lord rebuked us and told us to go to inner-city Hull and plant a Vineyard.'

Their team was only the two of them and their two young sons. No job to go to, just little scraps of work here and there, until the church grew enough to pay him. I remember speaking to him about it a couple of months ago, and he said, 'I was literally on the brink of really making it – directorship was surely beckoning.' But God spoke, so he left it all. He said to me, 'I have never once looked back and regretted that decision.' This is simply astounding to anyone who didn't know who he was following.

Let's go up to Scotland, to Peter and Rosemary Sturrock. Peter was a young partner in a law firm in Aberdeen. Peter and Rosemary encountered the Vineyard in 1987. God started to speak and stir their hearts. They decided that God was asking them to give up living in Scotland, which is hard for a Scot, and move to England – and for Peter to give up the partnership in the law firm. They moved to South West London Vineyard and started studying at London Bible College, after which they went to Redhill and planted a Vineyard church there. The journey took a few twists and turns. Essentially, it involved them going back to south-west London to support the Mumfords and then leaving it all again to go back to Scotland to plant another church there. What a story! All this happened because they were a couple who heard from God, and acted based on their trust in where he was leading them.

Now let's take a little leap across the Irish Sea, to Belfast, Northern Ireland. Andy and Harmony Smith lead Belfast City Vineyard. Their journey started in the USA, in Chicago. They were plugged into Steve Nicholson's church in Evanston and were just finishing Bible college when they felt called to ministry in Northern Ireland. Steve helped them to set up an internship in Belfast City Vineyard, which is the church that Evanston originally helped to plant. They raised their own support and took the risk. They weren't on the staff at Evanston, there was no job at Belfast; they went for it on a decent tide of prophetic confirmation. They didn't know that God would ask them to take on the church as senior pastors. They took that first, rather large, leap across the Atlantic. God's plan for them eventually became clear, step by step.

Do you notice a pattern here? I do. These are just a few of the stories we have here in the Vineyard. We've got well over 140 Vineyard churches in the UK and Ireland right now. That's more than 140 stories of gutsy, faith-filled women and men of God in this nation, in this Vineyard. But that's only the ones who planted the churches. There are also the ones who came with them on the church plants who served tirelessly.

For James and me – if we had not taken a team of absolutely extraordinary, servant-hearted, passionate Jesus followers with us – there is no way Cardiff Vineyard would be where it is right now; it was the people who made the effort and helped the church to grow – it was those who followed God into teaching, into community engagement, healthcare, politics and business. Then there were those who went overseas to take the gospel and meet needs in other parts of the world. We were and are truly surrounded by such a great cloud of witnesses.

Hebrews 11 is one of my absolute favourite chapters in the New Testament. In the same way that I wanted to tell you some of the early stories of the Vineyard in the UK and Ireland, this is exactly what Paul is doing in this scripture, far more eloquently, with the early Christians and with us. I once heard a wise man say, 'We should only be interested in the past, in so much as it helps us to learn for the future.' This is what this passage is all about. It's not about hearing all these great faith stories of how people have gone before us and thinking, 'Oh what a lovely story; weren't they great?' and just leaving it at that. This rousing passage is about something more – a kick-start, a friendly nudge.

I'm quite a visual person, so when I read the Bible I imagine a film scene coming to life. Paul is there in front of a room of disciples, the early pioneers of the Christian faith. Some of them are really encouraged and full of fire. But many of them are feeling tired and uninspired, scared even. I imagine there would have been a few empty chairs, left by those who had been persecuted and killed, from sharing the gospel or planting a church. There's nothing like someone's empty seat to remind you of the cost of what you're doing. So, Paul's up there thinking, 'I've got to remind them of the bigger picture. They need some models to follow. A reminder that they're not in this alone. It's been done before. People have done hard things before: they have trusted God with their lives, with their families, with their money, with their futures – all before. But by faith, only through faith.' So he launches into this passionate tirade of the old greats, telling their stories – by faith, by faith, by faith. Abel, Enoch, Noah and his crazy ark building. There's Abraham, who went somewhere he didn't know for someone he didn't know to start a people, who didn't even know how they came about because his wife was infertile and extremely old – the definition of wizened.

By faith, Isaac, Jacob, Moses, Joseph – Paul says, by faith. They did it all because of the Lord. Every story is by faith. This is the only motivator. Not safety, not good sense, not what everyone else is doing – by faith alone. Joshua and his trumpet-sounding, drum-banging army against every other army in the land. Rahab, David, Solomon. Then he ends with this:

> And what more shall I say? I do not have time to tell about Gideon, Barak, Samson and Jephthah, about David and Samuel and the prophets, who through faith conquered kingdoms, administered justice, and gained what was promised; who shut the mouths of lions, quenched the fury of the flames, and escaped the edge of the sword; whose weakness was turned to strength; and who became powerful in battle and routed foreign armies. Women received back their dead, raised to life again. There were others who were tortured, refusing to be released so that they might gain an even better resurrection. Some faced jeers and flogging, and even chains and imprisonment. They were put to death by stoning; they were sawn in two; they were killed by the sword. They went about in sheepskins and goatskins,

> destitute, persecuted and ill-treated – the world was not worthy of them. They wandered in deserts and mountains, living in caves and in holes in the ground.
>
> (Hebrews 11.32–38)

Then he goes on in chapter 12:

> Therefore, since we are surrounded by such a great cloud of witnesses, let us throw off everything that hinders and the sin that so easily entangles. And let us run with perseverance the race marked out for us, fixing our eyes on Jesus, the pioneer and perfecter of faith. For the joy set before him he endured the cross . . .
>
> (Hebrews 12.1–2)

We are truly surrounded by such a great cloud of witnesses – both from the ancient times but also here in this movement. We are resting on the risks and decisions made in faith, by those from the past. Now, it's our turn. The next chapter is yet to be written and it's up to you, to us, to write it. Our stories will be different from theirs. They have to be. There are now different challenges. There are different questions to be asked but the same route should be taken: by faith.

We are at a point where we can either carry on as normal or take a moment to reflect. Take a long deep breath and ask the Lord, 'What have you got for us, where are you leading us, what is my part to play in this next chapter?' What are we so afraid of? Because we are afraid, aren't we? Fear is one of the biggest things that hinders us.

Fear, when it clashes with faith, is one to watch. We all know that fear can be a really good protective instinct. We have been programmed from an early age to listen to it in order to save our skins. We've got to know, however, the difference between protective fear and faith-smothering fear. Fear in its very essence is a perceived threat. It's not the actual threat; it's the perception of what might happen. Good fear protects. There is a reason why when we stand at the edge of a cliff and look down, we start to tremble and sweat. That's our brains sending a message to our feet saying, please don't take another step, otherwise you might fall and die. Good fear drives us forward – like exam fear that drives you to work hard.

However, bad fear – faith-smothering fear – paralyses, smothers, lies and deceives us. This is what faith-smothering fear sounds like: 'If you do it, you'll fail and you'll look stupid and no one will respect you. If you do it, you'll never get paid enough. If you do it, you'll never find a wife and your children won't thrive. You can't do it anyway; you're not good enough, strong enough, clever enough. If you waste that many years of your life, you're going to regret not doing what your friends did. Why would God ask you to do that? You need a second opinion. Just wait until you've found a husband, wait until you've had children, wait until your children are older, wait until you've done the house up. Wait. Don't. Can't. Shouldn't.' Do you recognise that voice?

It's there, lurking in the back of all our minds. It's insipid and faith-smothering. You know whose voice it is? Satan. Whenever you sense Jesus is asking you to do something and this little voice starts whispering, you need to recognise it for what it is and banish it from your mind. 'Get behind me Satan.' Jesus once said that, didn't he? Sometimes, we have to say it with that ferocity. Do not let this voice get a foothold. Do not let this voice slow you down, turn you around, stop you taking the faith steps that Jesus is asking of you. Tell it where to go. Don't just do that. Replace it with faith. Remind yourself of what he said in the past and what he's saying now. Remind yourself of what you're sure you hope for and what you're certain of that you do not see. This is what faith sounds like: 'God said, so I am . . .'; or 'Jesus said, so I am . . .'

I think one of the biggest fears that young people have in this culture is not having enough money. If God asked you to change careers or retrain or even give up a day's work, if there's a drop in income, fear and doubt can creep in. 'How will I pay the mortgage or the rent, what about my holidays, pension . . . ?' I know that voice – it's always happened to me in the process of Jesus asking me to give up a career, give more or put things on hold. I know so many people who have not made decisions to follow what they sense God is asking them to do because of money. It's not even because they want loads of it. It's the fear of not having enough – but enough for what?

I was chatting with a friend of mine from church, Rachel. A year ago, she had just finished university and got married. She and her husband Dave came to our house to get our thoughts on what they sensed God was speaking to them about. They had both joined Cardiff Vineyard as students and, back then, Rachel hadn't quite understood why God wanted her to join. She'd always been really passionate about youth work – and at that time we probably had one or two members in the 11 to 18 age bracket, with absolutely nothing running for the young people.

Over this meal, they explained how they felt God could be asking them to live by faith that year, with Dave getting a part-time job and Rachel remaining unemployed so that she could plough her spare time and energy into getting something up and running for young people in the church and beyond – and that they would lead it together. Isn't that amazing? At the end of that evening, they left and we were like, 'Oh my goodness, if we have two people in our church with faith like that, surely a mustard tree could grow.' One year on, we have had a 1,250 per cent increase in our youth membership! There's a small youth group that runs weekly and it's better attended than the socials.

This is the Kingdom. It's the little steps, not knowing exactly where they will lead but being sure of what we hope for and certain of what we do not see. Rachel and Dave did live by faith that year – they lived off so little. There was this fear at the beginning of the year about how they were going to get by. I asked them how it had gone and she said, 'I don't know how, but through that entire year, we did not once go into our overdraft.' They made decisions like not getting a car, which, let's face it, is better for your health as well as the environment. They said no to things that they probably wanted to say yes to – but they ploughed their faith into what God was leading them into and he was with them.

Faith is being certain of what we hope for, what Jesus hopes for. But hear me right: I'm not saying don't ask questions. I'm not saying *blind* faith. That's not the sort of faith the Bible asks us to have. When we say things like, 'That sounds impossible, what you're asking me to do, Lord', if we press into the question, instead of abandoning the thought, something interesting happens.

So, we start with this: OK, I'm afraid of trusting God, I'm afraid that if I really lay down my life unconditionally for him, he'll let me down. Or we say: I'm afraid of trusting *me*. I'm afraid that if I give myself like this I won't be able to keep it up and I'll fail. There's often a combination of those fears. But if we press in and start to ask the deeper questions, this is the journey we go on. If I'm not trusting in what Jesus says then what am I trusting in? We'll each have slightly different questions and fears, but there's often common ground. We build our lives on cultural consensus, on public opinion. We build our lives on family, on economic security. In all these things, if we really look deeper, we know that these are not reliable.

For me the greatest irony of the past decade since the crash of the global financial market, which proves we can't put our faith in financial security, is this: we have become *more* obsessed with financial security than ever. Have we learned nothing? In fact, in every place, in all these things, God is saying: obey me and leave that behind. He's answering the call away from cultural, financial, relational, appearance, status security – over and over in the Bible. Why does God do that? It's because he knows we're going to build our lives on things that are going to go. Sand and not rock. God is saying to us, 'Don't build your life there, that has no foundation, that's sand. Don't centre life on that stuff.' There's a book by Timothy Keller called *Counterfeit Gods: When the empty promises of love, money and power let you down* (London: Hodder & Stoughton, 2010). It's an extremely honest look at the gods of our time. It's good to ask questions about what we're building our lives on. I urge you to follow the questions through. That's where we start to unearth the real truths about the values that we hold and the lies that choke us.

Put another way: it is OK to have fear. But it's what you say to it that matters. When I look through the stories of the Bible, I feel real comfort. I see all these heroes of the faith who were undoubtedly full of fear but followed God anyway. Why did God need to say continually to Joshua, 'Be strong and courageous'? If you've ever read Joshua, it's a bit like Hebrews. There's this phrase repeated: be strong and courageous. It's because Joshua needed to be continually reminded to have courage because God was with him.

When we step out for God we will vacillate between fear and faith. I promise you, it's the narrative of my life. Where does the path of fear take us? The heroes of the faith were just that because they were human enough to feel all the same emotions and think all the same thoughts as us – but they followed what God was leading them into anyway. A hero is someone who looks fear in the eye and says, 'God, I'm going to do it anyway.' Fear is OK. It's what we say to it that matters.

One more thing to mention about faith and fear is this. You've got to remember that when Jesus asks you to do something, to commit, to sacrifice, you're not alone. He has promised to be with us. He has promised that he will be with us until the end. He'll be awake when we're sleeping, with us through the darkest moments, leading us forward at each step. When I look back on my and James's journey, with each twist and turn, he's been with us. Jesus has only ever asked us to take one step at a time. We never knew what would happen when he asked us to leave everything we had in Nottingham, like our jobs and friends. James couldn't have loved his job more. God didn't promise us anything. All he said was, 'Leave in eighteen months and I'm with you.' And he was. He was with us in the first year of the church, when we grew and it was really exciting. He was with us in the second and third years of the church, when we felt like our worlds were falling apart – I had four miscarriages while we continued to lead the church and helped to launch the Cause to Live For conference.

We launched the first ever Cause to Live For gathering six weeks after my fourth miscarriage. I was signed off work with depression at the time. I remember so many Sundays during those two years, driving to church, pleading with God to help me. And he did. He got us through, limping and bruised, but through. Each step that he's asked of us, where we don't think we can take any more, he's promised he'll be with us. He is and he has been. I look at Cardiff Vineyard now and I see her faces, her history, I see people who know Jesus, people who have been carried through difficult times by her, people who have taken great leaps of faith and who are now thriving, children who are hearing God's voice and growing in their identity with him. It's been more than I dared hope for – and the next chapter is still unwritten. I'm trusting that God is leading us through every decision. I trust that he's with us and through it all he will be faithful. What else can we do but look forward to the city with foundations whose architect and builder is God?

The lessons from the past have to shape our decisions for the future. It's our vision for the future that has to inspire our futures. This is the visionary part of faith. God never asks us to truly walk into the unknown. He starts by placing a vision for the things unseen, in our hearts. These are the longings that it shouldn't be like this, if only that could happen. All the journeys of faith begin with a dream − something God places in our hearts. When we went to Cardiff, God gave us a vision. Moses had a vision − a God-given vision − to set the Israelites free. Joshua had a vision to lead them into the Promised Land. The Mumfords had a vision to start a movement of Vineyard churches in the UK and Ireland. Jeremy and Elaine had a vision for Hull; Rachel and Dave had a vision for young people in Cardiff. This stuff all starts with a faith-inspired vision of what God wants to use your life for.

Join with me in dreaming for a moment. What does this look like for you? From church planting to policy making to shaping our workplaces and friendship groups, choosing where we live, how we spend our time and money, which jobs to take. How are you making your decisions? Are you making them based on fear or faith?

Let me give you an example of something going on in our country that really bothers me. In the UK, current statistics reveal that 1 in 20 children have been or will be sexually abused, but the true figure is probably higher than this. You do not need to be a genius to know that this destroys lives. It's only one area of neglect; abuse and discrimination are going on right under our noses. Let me tell you something you'll also already know. It's those who have struggled through life − those with less, those at the lower end of the socio-economic ladder − who are much more at risk. I went to some child protection training a couple of months ago, and I sat there feeling sick and tearful and angry. We've got a lot better in this country at identifying and helping victims. But my big question is this: how can we stop this from happening in the first place? People might think, 'That's impossible, it's too embedded, too hidden, too complex – we'll never be able to stop that happening.' That's the enemy's voice again.

There's a woman who became head of police in Sweden and decided with her team to tackle prostitution, because of the link with the global sex trade. They began to look at who the women engaged in it are – mostly poor, marginalised and exploited – and what exactly they were doing. They considered the costs involved to the women: death, drug addiction, self-harm, post-traumatic stress disorder. Then they looked at the costs to society: policing, rehabilitation, medical treatments and the ever-increasing demand for more and more women. In a stunning and radical move, instead of criminalising the women, they changed the law and criminalised the men. Prostitution is no longer illegal in Sweden; visiting a prostitute is. They dealt with the demand rather than supply. Things have drastically changed in that country, more so than in any other nation. Gunilla Ekberg (a lawyer who was the Swedish Government's expert on prostitution and human trafficking) said that one of the key ingredients to getting to the truth, exposing the lie and changing a nation's mindset was the ability to imagine a different world, the ability to step outside the norm and picture a whole new truth.

That's not the first time a story like that has happened. Think of William Wilberforce and slavery. Think of the emancipation of women and the suffragettes. Those are the sorts of attitude-changing visions that God longs to breathe into so many of you.

A vision for a different world. A vision for his Kingdom in this nation. It's not just politics, policy, education and healthcare. It's church planting. Do you know why the Vineyard is so passionate about church planting? Because it really is only through the transforming power of the Holy Spirit that communities can be restored.

God sent James and me to Wales, which is where some of the most extraordinary moves of God occurred at the beginning of the last century. During the 1904 Welsh revival, it is estimated that a hundred thousand people flooded back to Jesus. Pubs were empty. For the duration of this revival, the nation of Wales was completely transformed. It wasn't just people turning back to faith. The by-products were that addictions were broken, crime was stopped, relationships and broken families were repaired, forgiveness and repentance became commonplace. This is what the overflow of the Holy Spirit looks like. It's not just the individuals transformed but communities and nations.

This is why we are committed to church planting – because when we plant a church, we are intentionally carrying the Spirit of God into a new community. What's the answer to the brokenness of our country, of this world? Put simply, carrying Jesus into every place by planting churches. There's a reason why Paul and Peter did that when they started the early church. There's a reason why statistically church planting is the most effective way of seeing people come to know Jesus. In order to do this, Jesus needs men and women who will stand up and take the call seriously and risk and trust and go. Just imagine what God could do with this country and beyond if all of us shrugged off the faith-smothering lies of the enemy and gave ourselves to dreaming of the different realities that Jesus longs to breathe into our hearts and minds.

What is it that God has been saying to you? What is it that the Holy Spirit has been whispering into your heart for years but you've been ignoring? Some of you have never asked him. You're fearful of what he might say, or what you might have to give up. Stop focusing on what you're going to lose and instead focus on what you're going to gain. Some of you were spoken to years ago and you ignored it. You filled your minds and time with box sets and social media and alcohol. You're wasting your lives. More to the point, you're wasting the life that God has given you. It's not actually yours, it's his. Have you asked him what he wants to do with it? There are people who are meant to church plant and you're dragging your heels. You know what God said – start training. There has never been a better time to train to plant a church. Some of you are meant to go on teams for church plants. Stop faffing around and worrying about jobs and houses and just go. They will come. Eighteen of us went to Cardiff. At the very beginning when we committed to go, none of us had homes or jobs. We went. God always provides. We've got to take that first leap. I dare you. When you catch this cause to live for, you will not regret it. Ups and downs – yes, absolutely – but the Kingdom of God is worth giving your life to.

Some of you don't know what God is saying. You feel confused. You're compromising in your lifestyles. Clean up your acts. Start desiring purity. Then you will see what happens, how God starts to speak. You won't have enough blank pages in your houses to write down all the heavenly encouragements that Jesus has to say to you, I can promise you.

Then there are those people who are called to start dreaming differently for the nation, to dream Kingdom values, into this land and others. Start believing in the dreams you've been given. Start listening to the Holy Spirit. Step by step, one act of faith followed by another. Who is going to stand up to things like child sex abuse and say 'not on our watch'?

You might be in the middle of a storm. You're going through it now because you're stepping out; you're tired and you need an arm around you, some prayer and encouragement. Let those who know and love you stand beside you and encourage and pray for you. Keep going. Keep pressing on towards the goal; remember who you're surrounded by. You know, our faith was built on the faith of men and women over thousands of years, making decisions and taking actions based on faith, not fear. In the past three decades, the Vineyard movement in this country has been formed by women and men taking decisions and actions based on faith not fear. Lives have been changed. Bodies have been healed. Hope has been restored. Communities have been put back together. All by faith in Jesus. Now it's over to you. I commission you. *We* commission you.

THE LOCAL CHURCH IS SUPPOSED TO BE LIKE A RAFT – A PLACE OF REFUGE WITHIN WHICH WE CAN NAVIGATE THE DIFFICULT WATERS OF LIFE.

Growth, health and forgiveness

Chuck Freeland

Chuck leads City Church Aberdeen with his wife Taryn and has a passion to see churches planted across Scotland.

Were you in the Scouts when you were a child, or in the Guides or both? The thing I loved most about being in the Scouts was the sense of danger; the sense that, as we were on trips or doing activities, something could go horribly wrong and somebody might lose their life as a result. The Scouts might have lost that sense of danger nowadays, but I hope they haven't. I remember a time when we were driven by minibus to the bank of a river. We got out of the van to find planks of wood, plastic barrels, bits of rope and life jackets on one side of the bank; a flag was on the other side of the river. 'What you need to do now,' began the Scout leader, 'is get into teams, build a raft, float across the river, get your flag and come back.' In no time at all we organised ourselves into teams, started strapping things together, put bits of plank on to barrels and thrust ourselves into the water. You can imagine what happened next! In even less time than it had taken to get into the water in the first place, the river was scattered with barrels and bits of wood and little Scouts with arms flailing in the air, life jackets up over our ears, in need of rescue.

'One, two, three, four.' We looked across the water, still bobbing around, to follow the faint sound of this chant. Soon, we saw the Scout leaders come into vision, floating effortlessly on this absolute beauty of a raft; it was like a seamless military manoeuvre. They went sailing past us, all the way to the other side of the river, picked up the flag and swung past, scooping us up on to the raft and returning us safely back to the bank.

'How did you do that?' we asked in awe.

The leaders replied, 'We knew this was going to be a difficult challenge so we spent as much time as we could thinking about how the raft would fit together. We knew certain bits of the raft would be under pressure and were likely to start to fall apart, so we put a double knot on it. We made sure that it was all connected as well as it could be. Then we started to get into the water.'

The reason I tell this story is this: the local church is supposed to be like a well-built raft. It is supposed to be a place of refuge within which we can navigate the difficult waters of life. It's supposed to be a place of safety, within which we can get into the flow of the Spirit of God, where we can find our way, going out into the nations. But not every raft makes it all the way to the end of the race. Just like our rafts in the story, not all churches find their way all the way to the end.

Let me explain further. My wife Taryn and I have been leading our church in Aberdeen for over seven years. No one was more surprised than we were when we found ourselves doing so. It wasn't what we had planned. But as we started to lead, God started to do amazing, ridiculous things. Again, no one was more surprised about that than we were! People started to come to faith and the church began to grow. Honestly, I wish I could pinpoint something we did that made all the difference. Every time I thought I knew why the church was growing, we did more of that and it made absolutely no difference or made it slightly worse. We've spent most of the past seven years saying, 'God, please don't let us get in the way of what you're doing. Please don't let us mess this up.'

Every now and then, the Lord does something to remind us, in case we were getting confused, that *he's* doing something, not us: that it's his grace and his kindness apart from our own. For example, a while ago, a man who'd been part of the Lithuanian mafia came to our church. He was running for his life from Lithuania and the mafia, and came to Aberdeen. One day, as he was walking along the street where our church was, he was overwhelmed by a sense of his own sinfulness and shame. He'd never felt it before; he later told us that he was so overwhelmed he felt he either had to throw himself under a bus or he had to ask somebody for help. He looked up and saw our church building. He came and knocked on our door. He said, 'Is there anything you can do to help me with my shame?'

We said, 'You'd better come in. There's nothing we can do to help you with your shame. But there is something that Jesus can do. In fact, he's already done it.' He became a Christian there and then.

It is an amazing story and we have many more to share like it! We have stories of people knocking on the door of our offices saying, 'Somebody told me about Jesus once about ten years ago and I've been thinking about it. Would it be all right if I came in and became a Christian now?' It's ridiculous. We don't know what we're doing. We're making it up as we go along. We have a strong sense of being complete idiots. However, God is incredibly kind to us. The Church, working together, can be like the Scout leaders on the raft, rescuing people from the river. But note how I say working *together*.

What we've realised, and continue to be reminded of, is that if our relationships break down, then the whole rescue plan of the Church could be dashed. For any of us who have been Christians for any length of time, we know that there are so many stories of churches serving the poor, reaching the lost, seeing people come to know Jesus, seeing remarkable things happening, exploding with growth – then relationships within the church break down and it's as if the church goes into meltdown. Sometimes they can come back from the brink. Sometimes they need help to come back from the brink. Sometimes they disappear without a trace and never return. I believe it grieves the heart of God that we don't do relationships better than we do. Sometimes it's a theological disagreement, sometimes it's a disagreement about the direction of the church, but ultimately what it comes down to is that two people, or a group of people, have fallen out and they don't know what to do.

During the years of leading a church, we've come to the conclusion that the single greatest threat to the Church's fruit-fulness in our generation is the one that the enemy poses to our relationships. The growth and health of the Church, while you and I are holding its reins, and hold some level of responsibility for it, rests not on our ability to be evangelistically effective or strategically brilliant or culturally relevant – but on our ability to love one another, to do life well with one another and to keep our relationships healthy. In other words, the ability of every raft – every local church – to make it all the way to the end of the race rests on the connections and the joins that make it up.

Several years ago, my wife Taryn had a complete emergency a month before Christmas: she'd run out of perfume! Coincidentally, my elderly grandmother had phoned up that week and said, 'I was wondering what Taryn wanted for Christmas?' What timing! This was the answer to the problem. So Taryn said she'd like (let's say, for the sake of argument) Clinique Happy. My mum then phoned up later that week to say she'd taken Grandma shopping and so the Clinique was in the bag. Phew!

Anyway, we get to Christmas and head down to visit the extended family – and I mean extended, there were some people there who were related to relatives of relations of our family! There were people we'd never seen before or since. I didn't even know their names! We started to pass around the presents. Taryn is holding this present from grandma as if it's worth a million pounds. She starts to open it, takes a deep breath and . . . it's a portable sewing kit. 'Oh, you shouldn't have,' Taryn says. *No, you really shouldn't have*, I think. Later, Taryn is passing a present that feels suspiciously like liquid to Hilda, or Bertha, or whatever her name was – clearly grandma had got a bit confused and Taryn's present had got mixed up with hers. Reluctantly, Taryn had to cross the room and give her Clinique Happy to Bertha. Not a very 'Happy' moment at all!

When it comes to our relationships, we can often feel like Taryn in this story. There is a gift that Jesus is calling us to give, abundantly and generously, and yet so many of us find it so hard to part with it. And that's the gift of forgiveness. It's actually the key to the Church being the Church, being fruitful for the long term, being in it for the long haul. It's our ability, as the people of God, to give away forgiveness.

Before we start to unpack the idea of forgiveness a little further, I have a confession to make. I'd rather not be talking about forgiveness – you have no idea how much the Lord and I have argued over the past few months about this subject. I can't get away from the fact that we – and by 'we' I mean the younger generation, even though I'm thirty-eight and many of you might not think that counts any more – have to figure this stuff out; it's incredibly important.

To help us better understand the central importance of forgiveness in relationships, we're going to have a look at Genesis chapter 45. In this scripture, we meet Joseph twenty years after his brothers have treated him with excruciating unkindness: they've beaten him, stripped him, put him in a pit – and they've sold him into slavery. This is the moment where Joseph chooses to give his brothers forgiveness:

> Then Joseph could no longer control himself before all his attendants, and he cried out, 'Make everyone leave my presence!' So there was no one with Joseph when he made himself known to his brothers. And he wept so loudly that the Egyptians heard him, and Pharaoh's household heard about it.

Joseph said to his brothers, 'I am Joseph! Is my father still living?' But his brothers were not able to answer him, because they were terrified at his presence. Then Joseph said to his brothers, 'Come close to me.' When they had done so, he said, 'I am your brother Joseph, the one you sold into Egypt! And now, do not be distressed and do not be angry with yourselves for selling me here, because it was to save lives that God sent me ahead of you. For two years now there has been famine in the land, and for the next five years there will be no ploughing and reaping. But God sent me ahead of you to preserve for you a remnant on earth and to save your lives by a great deliverance.

(Genesis 45.1–7)

We can learn a number of things about forgiveness from this example. First of all, *who* Joseph forgives, then *when* he forgives and *how* he forgives. But before we do, it's important to answer the question – why should we care? The simple answer is: forgiveness matters because it matters to Jesus. Uncomfortably, he talks about forgiveness a lot. In fact, I've come to the conclusion, having reviewed the teachings of Jesus on the subject of forgiveness, that you can say one thing with absolute certainty: my becoming a forgiving person is absolutely central to Jesus' plans and purposes for my life.

Not only did Jesus talk about forgiveness again and again and again, but so often he talks about it in what I like to call 'fridge-magnet verses' – verses that we read and love so much that we want to write them on fridge magnets and embroider them on doilies! These are the verses we want to chew on every day, because we know they'll do us good. Often when Jesus grabs his disciples' attention with these 'life verses', we find talk of forgiveness either immediately before or immediately after. Forgiveness is central to his purposes for us. Let me give you a few examples.

The first one is Mark 11.24. Jesus says, 'Therefore I tell you, whatever you ask for in prayer, believe that you have received it, and it will be yours.' That's a great verse isn't it? That's a real fridge-magnet verse. But how many of us have the very next verse embroidered on a doily? 'And when you stand praying, if you hold anything against anyone, forgive them, so that your Father in heaven may forgive you your sins' (Mark 11.25).

Another one – Luke 17.6: 'If you have faith as small as a mustard seed, you can say to this mulberry tree, "Be uprooted and planted in the sea," and it will obey you.' Immediately before this verse is this one: 'Even if they sin against you seven times in a day and seven times come back to you saying "I repent," you must forgive them' (Luke 17.4). Have you got that embroidered on a doily?

And another one – Luke 6.38: 'Give, and it will be given to you. A good measure, pressed down, shaken together and running over, will be poured into your lap. For with the measure you use, it will be measured to you.' Often we use this verse in the context of teaching about financial generosity. I'm sure this is a totally valid use of that verse. But Jesus isn't talking about finances. In fact, the previous few words are these: 'Forgive, and you will be forgiven', 'Give and it will be given to you'. You see, my sense is that we are reading Scripture selectively. By picking out the bits that we think are great verses, we avoid something else of incredible importance for us as disciples of Jesus.

Forgiveness is important because it is important to Jesus. Returning to Joseph and his brothers then, we can learn more about the nature of forgiveness. First of all: *who* he forgives. The Bible shows us that Joseph forgives his brothers. Who are his brothers? They eventually become the leaders of the twelve tribes of Israel. They are the family of God. I think the fact he forgives his brothers is hugely significant. Who are the family of God today? Of course, it's us. It's the Church. We have to be a community of grace. We have to be a community that lets one another off the hook – that forgives one another.

John Wimber said this: 'My brother is never my enemy. He's always my brother.' In our age, we need to hear that. In modern Western Christianity, when we experience difficult or broken relationships, we often say, 'Well, there's another church down the road. I'll go there instead.' We have options. I could leave a lot of churches and go to other churches. That is how too many of us in our society have learned to deal with difficult relationships – 'I'm going to leave this behind and move on to another one.'

Joseph forgave his brothers. The Lord's desire for us as the family of God is to figure this out. Not only did he forgive his brothers, he forgave his brothers who were the source of the greatest pain in his life – life-altering pain, pain that changed the course of his life. To be honest, I imagine we'd all have understood if he had said, 'Do you know what? Have some grain. I hope you choke on it. And just so you know, I'll never forgive you for what you did.' The reason we would understand him saying that is perhaps because this is the wisdom of our culture. In our society, it often feels like there is a line. Perhaps you lend somebody a box set and they don't give it back – maybe you can forgive that. Somebody always comes late for dinner when you invite them round. Maybe you can forgive that. Somebody reverses into your car. Well . . . that's where the line is – maybe you can forgive that, maybe you can't. But if somebody causes you life-altering pain, if somebody ruins your life, well, we don't do forgiveness for people like that.

What a good thing that Jesus didn't do things according to our wisdom and ways. It says in the Scriptures that, 'When they came to the place called the Skull, they crucified him there, along with the criminals . . . Jesus said, "*Father, forgive them, for they do not know what they are doing.*"' (Luke 23.33, 34, emphasis added). He forgave the men who were hammering nails into his hands.

I think Simon Ponsonby is one of the best Bible teachers around right now. I was listening to a podcast recently where he was talking about how he had written a book on moving in the power of the Holy Spirit and he then received around 150 invitations to talk about this topic. Then he wrote a book on holiness. He was invited to speak in about three churches. He reflected, 'Maybe we're not as interested in becoming like Jesus as we think we are.'

Jesus forgave the men who were driving nails into his hands. Joseph forgave his brothers, who had caused him life-altering pain. That's who he forgives. Second, we can learn from *when* he forgives. I've searched through the chapters that come before this and I can't find it; I can't find the apology. I can't find the moment when his brothers say to him: 'Joseph we're so sorry. We're sorry that we brutalised you. We're sorry that we hurt you. We're really sorry that we rejected you. We're sorry that we caused you all that pain.' They never said sorry. Yet he chooses to forgive them.

I think that's instructive for us. I've been a Christian for twenty-two years, and I've witnessed so many relationships break down. Often, you could take the person who caused the pain, strap them to a lie detector and ask them, 'Did you hurt them?' and they would reply 'No' and believe it; the needle wouldn't even flicker. There are people who cause pain wherever they go and honestly have no idea. If you're waiting for somebody to apologise to you before you forgive them, you might be waiting for the rest of your life. Don't wait for an apology.

It's also important for us to notice that it's now twenty years since they strapped Joseph to the camel. Here we see that it's never too late to forgive. You've probably heard people say things like 'To be honest, too much has been said' or 'There's too much water under the bridge' or 'It's too long ago now. It's too late.' The people who say that are completely wrong. It's never too late to forgive. Maybe that resonates with you right now. Maybe you've held on to bitterness and resentment against someone for a really long time. Maybe right now you can make a decision to leave that behind. You can be free – free from that bitterness and resentment that you carry around like luggage wherever you go. It's never too late to forgive.

I'm sure many of us have been inspired by the example of Nelson Mandela, who spent twenty-seven years in hard labour, crushing rocks with hammers for most of that time. Hilary Clinton recalls a conversation with Mandela about his release from prison. He told her: 'As I walked out the door toward the gate that would lead to my freedom, I knew that if I didn't leave my bitterness and hatred behind, I'd still be in prison' (*Living History*, New York: Scribner, 2004, p. 236). Joseph forgave his brothers after twenty years. That means for us it's never too late to forgive.

Lastly, we can learn from *how* Joseph forgives. The short answer is he forgives completely. He lets it all go. Taryn and I have three children. Our middle son Noah is really creative and he's the kind of child who likes making things out of stuff. He goes absolutely crazy if we try to throw away an ice cream tub he thinks he might be able to use to make something. It's as if we were trying to throw away something that's worth a million, trillion pounds.

Over time, we started to put things aside for him − the odd yoghurt pot here, the odd toilet roll there − into a little basket in our utility room. To say utility room makes it sound a lot grander than it is; it only has a tumble dryer and washing machine in it. Within no time at all, that cupboard of a room became what we affectionately called the 'plastic cupboard'. Now, if you've got children, you've got a plastic cupboard; I guarantee it. What happens is, you open the door and you get showered with plastic rain. After a while, it was getting really, *really* annoying. Taryn and I looked at each other and said, 'When he goes to nursery, we'll get a bin bag and throw a load of it away.' That's what we did, but we left a little bit of stuff there for him. The truth was, even the little bit left stopped us getting to the washing machine. It was still in the way, it was still annoying. And of course, over time, the pile of stuff began to grow until we were being covered in plastic rain all over again.

Eventually, I made a brutal decision. I got a bin bag while Noah was at nursery and put the basket, the tubs, the toilet rolls – everything, the whole lot – into it. Then Taryn and I did a little dance inside the utility cupboard, to celebrate the complete freedom that that moment had brought. Which is really sad, we know. My point is that Joseph didn't do half measures. He didn't forgive some of it but still hold on to some of it. He let go of it all. How do you know when you've forgiven completely? Well, there are a few indicators.

First, when no one else needs to know. Notice what Joseph does in Genesis 45.1: 'He cried out, "Make everyone leave my presence!" So there was no one with Joseph when he made himself known to his brothers.' Before we've arrived at a place of total forgiveness, what we do is – it may just be me – we phone up somebody and we say, 'You'll never believe what Gary did this week!' Then after a while, you'll be speaking to somebody in the coffee queue at church and say, 'That Gary – I'd give him a wide berth if I were you.' Then you'll be on Facebook and say, 'That Gary, he's a really nasty piece of work.' We are really happy to let everyone else know what other people have done. You know when you've completely forgiven someone when no one else needs to know. There is of course one exception to that: where a crime has been committed – then someone does need to know.

Second, you know when you've completely forgiven someone when your heart is soft. Verse 2 says: 'He wept so loudly that the

Egyptians heard him.' His tears signified the fact that he was no longer wearing armour around his heart, that his heart was soft towards his brothers.

Lastly, you know when you've completely forgiven someone when there can be proximity without pain. Joseph demonstrates that he has completely forgiven his brothers when he says in verse 4, 'Come close to me.' To be honest, as I've been reflecting on all this stuff, this is where the rubber really hits the road in my life. The truth is, my church is really nice to me – but I know this isn't the case for a lot of pastors, who get mentally beaten up in the post. As I've been preparing this teaching, I've felt the Lord reminding me of a person who was in my life years ago. I used to meet up with him and he would speak into my life. I would be vulnerable with him and he'd help me to work out what it means to follow Jesus. I was a young Christian. I don't know what really happened but there was a series of unfortunate events, which ultimately led to a moment where I felt completely crushed by him. It was probably my fault but it felt like he'd taken my soul out of my body and put it on the floor and stamped on it.

Just recently, I saw this guy at a conference. And it was as if it had all happened yesterday. I was completely horrified. I said to Taryn, 'I can't believe that these emotions have stirred within me; I feel completely torn up inside.' I really thought I'd dealt with it. Taryn turned to me and said, 'There's a world of difference between forgiving someone and avoiding them.' You'll know when you've forgiven someone completely when you can still be near them and you can bless them. Joseph's forgiveness is complete forgiveness.

What is the result of letting people off the hook, even though they've caused you life-altering pain? You would think that the result would be regret: 'I can't believe I've let them off the hook. I've made a terrible decision.' But actually, the result of forgiveness is never regret. It's always *relief*. Genesis 45.14 says, 'He threw his arms around his brother Benjamin and wept, and Benjamin embraced him, weeping. And he kissed all his brothers and wept over them.' He's not weeping because he feels regret. He's weeping because he's so relieved.

Years and years ago, I had a *proper* job. I worked in a software company, near London Bridge station. After I had been working there a little while, I walked into the office to find a parcel on my desk. I opened it to find a mobile phone. After about two years of using this phone, I came into the office one day and there was another phone there; they called it an upgrade. I asked them what I should do with the old phone, and they said I should throw it away. Since then I've had many mobiles. You see, we live in a disposable culture; we keep things for a while and then throw them away. Nothing lasts for ever. And many of us have started to do that with relationships. But do you know what? Jesus often said to his disciples, 'Not so with you.'

If we want to have marriages that last, friendships that last, ultimately if we want to have churches that last, we have to get really, really good at saying 'I'm sorry'. We have to get really, really good at learning to forgive. Only then will our bonds and ties be tight enough to steer our well-built raft through choppy waters and bring people safely back home.

WE HAVE A REASON TO
LIFT OUR EYES WITH AN
AUDACIOUS HOPE THAT
WE ACTUALLY MIGHT
BE ABLE TO MAKE A
DIFFERENCE.

Worshipping with wounds and swords

Miriam Swaffield

Miriam helps to equip the student church for mission around the world through her work with Fusion, an organization that supports students in the work of evangelism.

Some of the most profound things I have learned about justice and mission come from hanging around Vineyard pastors. I remember when Gary Best, who planted the Vineyard in Canada, spoke to me after spending twelve days renovating a house for the poor. Their builder had simply walked off site, leaving the work paid for but incomplete. So Gary, using more of his own money and borrowing other people's, had to renovate this house for the homeless on his own. 'Miriam,' Gary said to me, 'this nearly broke me but, the thing is, Jesus said, "Love the poor." He didn't say it wouldn't be hard, he said love the poor. So I'm going to show up because that's what I've been called to do.' Incredibly challenging. That's part of the Vineyard's DNA. Another Vineyard leader, David Ruis, has 'consider the poor' tattooed on his arm. It's part of the Vineyard's DNA. So I wasn't surprised when I was asked to teach on the topic of worship and justice.

Truth be told, I've been raised as a Christian, so my understanding of worship can be tainted by the fact I've always been part of the church community and always followed Jesus. It's almost not that fresh to me or cutting edge, it's part of what we do. I can also be very quick to put it in a box and stereotype it.

The other night, I was putting my godson, Morgan, to bed. He always likes to hear a song before he goes to sleep. A little bit like Christian karaoke or a jukebox, he requests things. Annoyingly, he had just had a harvest assembly, so he was all about harvest. It was really irritating because we don't sing about harvest apart from in primary schools. So, I'm wheeling out any classics I can remember from my Church of England primary school. Morgan isn't really impressed by it. He says, 'Can you sing me one that Mummy and Daddy haven't taught me?' I'm struggling here. But Morgan and I had been reading about wildlife, so I thought he'd love 'The Lion and the Lamb'. So I start singing. I'm making up the actions as I go. I try to make it into a children's song. I finish the chorus and I've really gone for it. At the end, all he has to say is, 'Is that it? Bit short.' I tell him to go to bed, it's a school night.

How do we define worship? How do we see worship? I know the theology of it – that we live a lifestyle in worship to God; that we're poured out like a drink offering. Our life is a song of praise to him. But realistically, if I think about being a good worshipper, it's stand up, arms up, sing up.

Having been raised in church, when I think about worship, I can't help but think of the stereotype of, 'Now we're going into a time of worship' and that's always somehow related to music and song.

If you're really into it, your eyes are closed and your arms are in the air. That's it? It's a crisis of theology and creativity if that is the pinnacle of what it means to be a worshipper. If that's what it means to be a good worshipper, I'd have to discount myself from being any good at it or called to being one. I get very easily distracted. I get distracted by whoever's attempting to sing next to me. Either that or my arms get tired. What a nightmare. I'm not a good worshipper if that's what worship is.

We can do the same thing with justice. Just as we can limit worship to 'stand up, arms up, sing up', we can restrict what it means to be a person of justice too. Realistically, where does my mind go when I think of Christians as a people of justice? I think . . . outsource it. Set up a standing order to something that promotes justice. I think of organisations rather than churches. Not that there's anything wrong with that but I immediately put it somewhere else. I think of an event or a campaign – I can do something then I can tick my justice box. Or I will go and ask the vegetarian in church who is the only one really living ethically among us.

I've packed worship into a musical box; I've put justice into an outsourced social action box, instead of making eye contact with a homeless person, finding out their name and offering to pray with them. Instead, my actions should match up with what I preach. We need to let what we believe and profess overflow into every area of our lives so that we actually stand up for the person who's getting bullied; so that we actually notice and start to pray, 'Lord, who in our midst is being trafficked?' – because in most of our cities, that is a reality now. Rather than turn a blind eye and outsource it and hope somebody else does it.

My friend Freya and I used to prayer walk the streets of York. York is not known for human trafficking but we thought, if we're justice people and this is the patch on our watch, then the least we can do is begin to walk and pray, particularly in the areas of town that are known for brothels and students engaging with that. We started to walk around different areas of the city. It made us pay attention when, years later, the police started to uncover things just down the road from us. I wonder whether those miles walked and those prayers prayed might have made a difference — because we're justice people who didn't outsource it to someone else. What does it look like to be a justice person?

Now I have a bit of a random passage to bring to you. This isn't a passage about worship or justice, not overtly. But it really helps me to engage with the question: how do I become a living, breathing temple of the Holy Spirit, in such a way that the way I walk is pouring out my worship to Jesus? And being so conscious of the justice of God that I stand up for the oppressed and the poor and the suffering — because it is in his nature and he lives in me so it must be in mine.

In 2 Corinthians 4, we meet our mate Paul. He's a hero of the New Testament, did a whole lot of church planting and then supported those churches. In this passage, he's writing to the Church in Corinth but he's aware that his teaching would have gone to surrounding areas too. Although it was written for a specific community, like all Scripture it's God-breathed. Pay attention to what he says because it gives us a really powerful picture of how Paul understood walking out the promise of God. This is what he says:

For what we preach is not ourselves, but Jesus Christ as Lord, and ourselves as your servants for Jesus' sake. For God, who said, 'Let light shine out of darkness,' made his light shine in our hearts to give us the light of the knowledge of God's glory displayed in the face of Christ.

But we have this treasure in jars of clay to show that this all-surpassing power is from God and not from us. We are hard pressed on every side, but not crushed; perplexed, but not in despair; persecuted, but not abandoned; struck down, but not destroyed. We always carry around in our body the death of Jesus, so that the life of Jesus may also be revealed in our body. For we who are alive are always being given over to death for Jesus' sake, so that his life may also be revealed in our mortal body. So then, death is at work in us, but life is at work in you. It is written: 'I believed; therefore I have spoken.' Since we have that same spirit of faith, we also believe and therefore speak, because we know that the one who raised the Lord Jesus from the dead will also raise us with Jesus and present us with you to himself. All this is for your benefit, so that the grace that is reaching more and more people may cause thanksgiving to overflow to the glory of God.

Therefore we do not lose heart. Though outwardly we are wasting away, yet inwardly we are being renewed day by day. For our light and momentary troubles are achieving for us an eternal glory that far outweighs them all. So we fix our eyes not on what is seen, but on what is unseen, since what is seen is temporary, but what is unseen is eternal.

(2 Corinthians 4.5–18)

That scripture alone, even if I didn't say anything more, could have a transformative effect on the way that you walk, worship, love and see the power of God in you. I know this because that scripture transformed my life and I've never heard it preached on. This became like an anchor, a touchstone, a point of reference and a steadying point for me when Mum and Dad got divorced while I was at university. This became a real place of finding hope and understanding how I could stand and worship, how I could walk with hope, how I could love and serve people that were broken and oppressed, even though I myself felt broken and let down.

This passage anchored me. I used it as my touchstone when one of my best friends got cancer. We had a year's worth of journeying through that. Again, I came back to these words of Paul and this idea of still carrying treasure even though I felt really like a broken and battered jar of clay. This scripture causes me to fix my eyes on Jesus. It lifts my perspective to the eternal. It helps me live a life that is a poured-out sacrifice of worship to God, so conscious of others who suffer around me, even in the midst of storms.

There's so much in this scripture, but I want us to pay attention to a few things right now. The kind of worship Paul describes isn't the kind that says stand up, arms up, sing up. However, understanding this passage means you can't help but declare the glory of God. I also love the fact that this passage doesn't put Christians in the best seat in the house.

What I think can happen with justice and social action is that we accidentally come across as the strong and sorted ones who need to go and help the ones who aren't sorted, to do something to and for somebody else. Whereas Paul puts us firmly in the place of the walking wounded. He knows that being a Christian and carrying this treasure means you're also walking with a limp. Following Jesus guarantees suffering. Following Jesus guarantees trouble. Yet somehow Paul has found this secret of living out as a sacrifice of worship, praise and glory – despite his circumstances.

I sometimes get sick of people quitting faith in their late twenties, early thirties or even at university because it got too hard. What did you think you were signing up for? When you look at the teachings of Jesus, it couldn't be clearer that you're signing up to take up your means of death and shame, to pick up your cross and follow him. He makes it super clear before he leaves the earth that in life we will have trouble, but we should take heart and have courage because he has overcome the world. Jesus himself is the suffering King.

We start to refine what worship means, and what justice means, when we are victims of injustice and when we don't feel like worshipping. I would love us to be a generation who knew what we signed up for – and we signed up for the cost as well as the glamorous bits. We signed up for life but we knew that meant death. I would love it if we carried this on into our thirties and there were more of us. Not only would we take the whole gospel seriously but we would tell our mates, so we'd expand the Kingdom, not by gift wrapping the gospel but by telling the whole truth: this is life, true life, real life, whole life, the only life, but it will also cost you your life, your entitlement, your sense of being sorted and being able to help other people. No, actually, we're in weakness and God is strong. Jesus is the suffering King and we are his servants.

Do you see how this starts to shift our perspective on worship and justice? Automatically, this passage doesn't leave Christians in the strongest seat in the house. In fact, we're the victims of injustice, yet we're called to pour ourselves out for others.

There are a few things I want to highlight here. First, we have this treasure in jars of clay to show that this all-surpassing power is from God and not from us. Have you seen the list that Paul says they're going through right now? Hard-pressed, oppressed, persecuted, struck down and carrying death as well as life. We are the walking wounded but we are wounded warriors.

God never disqualified anybody because they felt too weak. In fact, that was often the moment he called them and said, 'It's OK because I'm strong.' It's not about your strength; it's about the strength of him that lives in you. It's not about your power; it's about the power of the one that raised Jesus from the dead living in you. It's not about how you feel or whether you feel like worshipping. It's about pouring out worship because of him that lives in you, who sacrificed for you and still demands everything that you are and all that you have, even in the midst of suffering.

Your weakness is your strength. Your death is your life. It's that weird Kingdom tension and juxtaposition. Even when you don't feel like it, declare that God is good and that his presence lives in you; worshipping breaks chains and brings freedom. You can be a suffering servant exactly as you are. You have unbelievable power because Jesus is living in you. You yourself without him are just a clay pot, an empty jar that needs to be filled. We've got nothing without him.

The call to worship in this passage is a call of a Christian bleeding and beaten, Paul on his knees in prison, looking up and remembering that Jesus lives, remembering that he overcomes. Jesus is on his throne, he is in eternity and therefore we can stand and worship. We can celebrate when other areas of the Church are doing a phenomenal job while ours is finding it really tough. We don't get too proud when the Vineyard's exploding and we don't get too arrogant when our area of life seems to be going so well, because we know another bit of the body is suffering. We worship together and contend for one another because it's not about what you feel like or not, how good you are, it's about who lives in you, pouring it all out.

Second, the Kingdom is now and not yet. And in the same way, I would say that justice is now and not yet, because the Kingdom will bring everything right. It will bring justice. When Jesus finally gets to be King on earth as in heaven, and makes all things right, there will be no more injustice. So we know the Kingdom is coming and it has come. It is both in us and it is still to arrive.

When you look at this passage, you realise that's exactly what the early Christians are going through. Literally, Paul is saying, 'I am currently dying and I celebrate that you are living. I am currently beaten and oppressed and I celebrate that more and more people are worshipping God because they're meeting God.' He is living in that tension right now. We all live in that tension, don't we? Justice has come and the Kingdom is coming.

And then it's not yet, isn't it? Because you're still walking past that homeless friend and you know their name and you have a chat. Honestly, addiction is still biting. They can't seem to shake it and you don't know what to do, because you can't take them home to your student house but you're a bit lost about what to do about that. It's tough because, just by living in this country and walking down our high street and wearing the clothes from that high street, we know there is the blood of children on them. The fashion industry is so screwed up – sweatshops are everywhere and we don't know what to do about that now. We know there is incredible waste going on. We know that climate change is ravaging the poorest places which were already struggling.

The Kingdom is not yet; justice has not fully arrived. You can see how you can walk with a limp – a wounded warrior – because it is hard and it hasn't all been made new; and yet we have a reason to lift our eyes with an audacious hope that we actually might be able to make a difference. We have this unshakeable faith that, if we pray, something might be overturned in the physical and spiritual. We honestly believe that there is more, that there is another way, that everything will be made new. That's why we share it. Because this isn't enough. We know the Kingdom is coming. We know that justice is available and possible. But we're not there yet.

A true understanding of the justice of God is a reason why we can worship. When we feel it and when we don't; when we're a victim of injustice and when it's something we see around us. We can worship anyway – because not only is the Kingdom breaking in now but we know that Jesus will make it all right in the end. Jesus has won, is winning and will win. That means we can worship, even if we don't feel like it or see it in our own context. He's on his throne and he is King and he will come back again. It's a reason to worship.

Finally, the reason we can still worship is because of this eternal perspective. This is really hard for our generation. We're so instant that we're barely present because in so many different ways we're trying to be present in other people's lives while we're not truly present in our own. So the very idea of having an eternal perspective is a huge challenge in our culture. It'll be offensive to your friends if you say you're content and you have enough. Some of the most offensive things you can say to our culture at the moment: I have enough, I have peace and in God I am content.

Extraordinary, just flying against the culture that says you need a little bit more of that, a little bit less of that, consume, consume, throw away what you don't want, move on to the next thing, climb the ladder, compare yourself to everybody around you, scroll the Facebook feed and notice how everyone is happier than you, then try to buy your way into more of that happiness. Comparison is robbing our joy. Mental illness in our generation is sky-rocketing. Last year alone, York University had seven suicides – it hasn't been that many for the past ten years. Our society is breaking us. We are breathing in carbon monoxide we can't even see. It's robbing us of an eternal perspective and hope in Jesus.

The instant isn't satisfying but that's all we've got; we seek what we want and what we feel like, dispose of what we don't need any more. But we can walk differently, because we're a different people from a different Kingdom. We're wounded but we're warriors. We know justice is now and not yet, and we have an eternal perspective.

You see how Paul can walk through being beaten, bleeding, dying? Because he says we fix our eyes not on what is seen but on what is unseen, for what is seen is temporary but what is unseen is eternal. A life of worship is a life that is postured towards eternity and then lives out the present with that in mind. That completely changes the way you love people, how you pray, where you put your money and time, your level of hope and contentment, as well as giving you a hunger for more than you see. There should be an urgency when you come to look at eternity because you know it's coming and you also know the friends who don't know about it yet – we know where home is but we have an open invitation.

An eternal perspective means that when we worship – standing up, arms up, eyes closed, singing out – when we go into that kind of worship, we are actually joining in with angels. You are seeing a little glimpse of what it might be like, because we have an eternal perspective – and that means yes, you can be broken and bleeding and you can still walk, and still have hope, still stand and worship, even on the days when you don't feel like it.

It's a choice, that's what I'm learning. The presence of God in me, the overflow of him, means it should spill out into every area of my life. But I can be open and invitational about that or I can build up walls and worship on a Sunday in a set environment, safely among Christians, then live like everyone else on a Monday to blend in.

The Spirit of God is in us but it's up to you to give him permission to flow all the way through you and out of you. It means that, on the difficult days – when your parents break up, when your mate gets cancer, when you fail all your exams, when you don't know what to do when you graduate, when marriage is really hard, when the children thing is really tough, when career dreams aren't what were promised – in those moments, that's when it kicks in. Are you going to feel entitled or are you going to fight for other people's justice? Are you going to stand up for the poor even though you feel bad, and stand up for the ones that Jesus is close to? Will you worship when you feel like it or will you worship because you know that in eternity every knee will bow, every tongue will confess that Jesus is Lord?

We're jars of clay. Isn't it extraordinary that God will put his treasure in us? Isn't it extraordinary that he would choose to put his power rooted and embodied in the Body of Christ in us – then say, 'Go, pour out your life in worship to me'? Because the Spirit of the sovereign Lord is on you and you are good news to the poor. You will see prisoners set free. You will see captives released. This is the day of the Lord's favour and you carry his treasure to work that out.

I pray that the Holy Spirit gives you an eternal perspective and you choose to stand in worship, whether you feel like it or not. Some of you will feel like victims of injustice. Some of you will feel so overwhelmed by some of the stuff going on in the world, that you feel disempowered. I pray that the power of God will remind you of him who lives in you. It's not your job to save the world – Jesus has already done that – but you get to be a door holder to his Spirit and his way. I pray that the amazing scripture in 2 Corinthians 4 is your touchstone, that it is your go-to in some of your storms. I pray that it helps you to live a life of justice and worship – in any context, season and story past your twenties.

Therefore we do not lose heart. Though outwardly we are wasting away, yet inwardly we are being renewed day by day. For our light and momentary troubles are achieving for us an eternal glory that far outweighs them all. So we fix our eyes not on what is seen, but on what is unseen, since what is seen is temporary, but what is unseen is eternal.

(2 Corinthians 4.16–18)

Father, give us your perspective, so we might be a people that live a life of worship and justice. Holy Spirit, help us live from an eternal perspective. In Jesus' name we pray. Amen.

WHEN YOUR HEART IS SOFT, ANYTHING CAN HAPPEN. THAT'S WHEN GOD HAS YOU IN THE PERFECT PLACE.

Worship and justice

Ben Cooley and Martin Smith

Ben is the co-founder and Chief Executive of Hope for Justice, an anti-slavery and anti-trafficking organisation working to bring an end to modern slavery, and the author of *Impossible Is a Dare* (London: SPCK, 2017). This interview was recorded in 2016. For the latest news from Hope for Justice, visit <hopeforjustice.org>.

Martin is a singer and songwriter, known for being the frontman of Delirious? and for his gift of leading worship around the world.

We'd love to take a snapshot of your stories. Could you start by saying where you're from, a bit about your families and also how you met Jesus?

Ben Cooley: I grew up in the North-East. Though my parents have always believed that miracles and healings can happen today, my mum and dad found themselves at a church that started speaking against the Holy Spirit and about how the Holy Spirit was only around in biblical times. So they left with a couple of other families and started a church in the North-East of England called Emmanuel. It grew quite quickly, and ended up with about eight or nine hundred people in it. It was a dynamic church that saw people gain salvation every week – it was amazing growing up in it. My mum and dad always allowed me to be eccentric – they didn't squash it out of me. My dad allowed me to be audacious and dream big. I am a by-product of that. I moved to Manchester to train as an opera singer and met my wife, Debbie.

When I moved out of Manchester, I started leading worship in a small local church of about three hundred people. I was volunteering for an event run by a woman called Marion White. I walked into the building and I heard about the issue of modern slavery. Millions of people are currently caught in slavery – 1.2 million children a year are sold, that's two children every minute. I walked out of that building that night and thought, 'If that was my daughter, I would do something.' The next thought changed the course of my life: they are all someone's daughter and I should do something. So I did what any impassioned twenty-six-year-old would do: I booked the NEC Arena. I didn't know anything about putting on an event! I asked my dad to pick up Jon Foreman (the frontman for Grammy Award-winning rock band Switchfoot) from the airport and I had my child's stuff in the car and didn't know you needed to 'host' people. I had this audacious dream to raise awareness about modern slavery and, thanks to people like Martin supporting me, and Tim Hughes (the worship leader and songwriter), we had almost six thousand people attending our first event.

So Martin, tell us about your journey of faith . . .

Martin Smith: My mum and dad are Christians – great upbringing, great family. But it was very non-charismatic. I was brought up in a church called the Brethren Church, a tiny little chapel with 80 people. We had never really heard about the Holy Spirit or miracles. I remember my grandfather sitting down and talking about how miracles are not for today. I remember him looking me in the eye and saying, 'Don't believe any of that stuff.' Having said that, they're really godly, faithful people. It was only when I left home when I was seventeen that I started going to a church in Eastbourne. It was this crazy church where people were lifting their hands. I thought it was amazing. I knew deep down that this was great and I knew they had something I didn't. That was a fantastic journey for me. While I was there, one of the guys said, 'Have you ever led worship?' I didn't really know what he meant. He said, 'Can you do it this Sunday?' I felt the Spirit of God on my life. Sometimes that's enough, isn't it? Then all the rest comes in time. I met my wife shortly after that and she was part of this crazy charismatic church on the south coast, near Littlehampton – so I married into that. Her dad was running the church and that was the birth of a series of recordings by Delirious? called *Cutting Edge*.

Both of you have touched on the whole idea of calling. Could you explore that a little bit? How do we get a calling? How do we begin to walk out our calling and vision for our lives? What are some lessons you've learned in all that for us to listen to?

MS: I think that sometimes it can be a little bit simpler than that. If each of us looks across our day and thinks about what we've done for most of that day – or over a week – whether you're a reader, a pray-er, or you like being outdoors, or watching TV or movies. Think about the thing that you naturally love doing the most and I would say that's probably something to do with your calling because, if we follow the premise that God doesn't mess up when he makes us, then there's probably a reason you love doing that thing. Look to the thing you naturally buzz about. The reason you buzz about it is because God has put it inside you. That is what makes it unique for each of us. When you go on that track, then life actually becomes really easy. You'll end up doing what you love and doing it for God – he's called you to it anyway, so there's nothing to worry about.

BC: One of the greatest challenges is starting. God can inspire us with ideas for our lives but it's the first step that's often the hardest. How do I make a start? Looking back at the early days of Hope for Justice now, if I was going to book an arena, I would be panicking. It's amazing how wonderful a lack of knowledge about something like that is – at the time. After the arena event, it was actually just me in my small office with a wonky desk and a single phone. I think many things start off small – and that's OK. That's why the Bible says do not despise the day of small beginnings. Calling can start small. It doesn't have to be on a massive platform. For many it starts small, and then gradually builds up little by little.

If we think about what vision means, someone – I can't remember who – said, *a vision is a view of a preferable future.* A visionary needs to learn to separate their long-term vision of the future from the goals they set for the interim – things they need to achieve in order to get there. It's that tension between the 'now' and the 'next'. A visionary always looks at the next and is always frustrated because they're not living in the next. When I started Hope for Justice, I dreamed of having two offices. That was my next: if I had two offices, two locations and was rescuing hundreds of people, that would be awesome. By the time I got that, I was dreaming of five offices. By the time I got to five, I was dreaming of fifteen offices. It's that little by little – and it's celebrating the now. I think how someone copes with their calling is to tackle it little by little, but more importantly by celebrating the now. The now you are living was previously your next.

So, in terms of living in the now, can you tell us a little about the projects, what they look like for you? For you, Martin, being involved in worship, what are you up to at the moment? What does it look like to be living out this calling at the moment?

MS: I think that's the amazing thing about God: it's always moving. You never get to a point in your life, or you should never get to a point in your life, where you think, 'I've done it. Look at all these things God has blessed me with, now I can chill out and play golf or whatever.' It's not like that with God. Calling is almost as if your life will collapse if you don't do it. God's got you so tightly. You're so enthralled that you cannot wake up the next morning unless you're pursuing what your heavenly Father is asking you to do. So it gets more and more and more – there's not a point where it stops.

So, for me I guess, my life started with a prayer. I was thirteen years old, sitting in church, in a very, very traditional church, with a lady playing the church organ. She was amazing by the way; I'm not criticising that. But I was thinking, 'If my friends from school ever came to this, they would die – and I would die.'

I prayed an audacious prayer: God, if there's any way I could be involved in church music, that I could help my friends at school like it. It was a really simple prayer at thirteen years old. I set my course on that and I've never changed from that course.

There are seasons where it's all big and you feel like you're influencing a lot of people. There are seasons where you lie low – the past six or seven years have been like that, where I'm transitioning into something new. Teaching new stuff. I've got teenage children. There's more to my calling now than just music, does that make sense? I'm trying to be a good husband, lead new things at church. It goes on and on.

That prayer about wanting godly music to touch people outside the Church would be what's running through my veins. That hasn't stopped. We're in another season where, on a good day, you can say that there are some incredible songs being written right now. The best ever in the history of Christian music. There are some incredible songs. On a bad day, I could think, this is really boring now, the whole scene. That's not me being judgemental or critical – that's just my own reaction to it. I'm thinking, OK, where are those fourteen- to seventeen-year-olds out there who are going to turn this thing on its head again? We've been doing what we've been doing for twenty years now. Drums, bass – it's fine, there's nothing wrong with it. But you're probably having those same conversations that I was when I was thirteen. This is OK but we feel there's something new coming. I'm probably not going to be that person now who's going to bring that fresh thing. I can't really do that in the same way. I can encourage it and get behind it. In my own small way, I can put my money where my mouth is.

I have another musical project called Army of Bones; it's a bit more mainstream – we're going into small clubs with sticky floors. We're trying to be a light there, in our own small way. For me, it's the same thing: taking the presence of God to those places where I'm able to go. I probably couldn't do that with 'I Could Sing Your Love Forever' or 'Waiting Here For You' – but I can do that with another set of songs, which talk about how I've struggled in different areas of my life, pain and marriage and that sort of stuff. I can talk about that there.

I think we've been brought up with a theology where, if God gives you a gift, it's sanctified and it's basically just for church. Actually, I think the greatest sanctification of our gift is that it's for the world. It's not only for a Sunday morning meeting, is it? I think there needs to be an explosion of this slightly different attitude, where the important thing is not only making church better but also how this affects your world, your culture – it's not about getting people feeling more on a Sunday morning. I love leading worship in church. It's a great passion of mine, but my heart is also to let people who wouldn't normally come to church experience something of who God is.

Ben, tell us about the projects you're involved in at the moment. Tell us about Hope for Justice and what that looks like.

BC: At Hope for Justice, we've got to a point where we employ investigators and lawyers and social workers. In the UK, we have three centres. We work predominantly with victims who don't want to engage with law enforcement agencies because they come from an area in the world where there is disreputable policing. They don't trust law enforcement. So we help them.

We learned through West Yorkshire Police that 61 per cent of victims we rescued in 2012 went to the police during their abuse and were turned away; they were told it was a civil matter. West Yorkshire is the fourth largest police force in the country, right. So we decided we would step up, step out and set up an office there. In the first year of operating in Bradford, we rescued 110 victims of modern day slavery – the youngest was three months old and the oldest fifty-eight years old. Of that total, thirty-three of them came from a factory that was making beds for some of the largest retailers in the UK. We went to the Police and Crime Commissioner in that area and said, there is a significant problem, can we help serve you, we're going to continue helping individuals who don't want to engage with law enforcement but we want to help you. So we offered him three things. One: to train all his front-line officers on how to identify victims of human trafficking and how to deal with victims of that crime. In a four-month period, we trained more than 4,800 police officers in groups of 50. Second, we set up a network in that area talking about where there were gaps in that system and why prosecution rates were so low. Third, we set up a memorandum of under-standing with West Yorkshire Police, where we would work on every single one of their cases and they would work on our cases. True partnership, collaboration. It's amazing how far you can get when no one cares who gets the credit. In a year of operating in that area, we increased the rescue rates by 119 per cent in that city. We did that again in the West Midlands last year. We launched an office in Birmingham. We increased the rescue rates by 127 per cent – rescued 103 people. We're seeing that and we're taking that model across the globe. We launched that in Stavanger, Norway. Then we expanded into the USA two years ago.

A few years ago, I was in Virginia Beach on a TV show, with a panel talking about human trafficking. There was a guy next to me from the FBI and he was arguing with me about how an NGO shouldn't do what we do. We exchanged business cards afterwards. When he emailed me, I saw on the bottom that he was the head of all FBI efforts on human trafficking, nationally and internationally. I subsequently found out that he reported through to Barack Obama – which intimidated me. You should find out who you're arguing with. My dad always taught me, don't start a fight you can't finish.

The FBI guy said, 'Can you come over to the USA? I want to talk to you about what you're doing.' I flew over to Washington DC and he grilled me for three hours. Then he turned to me and said, 'Ben, my wife and I have been praying and the Lord's told me I have to come and serve under your leadership.' He left the FBI and came on staff at Hope for Justice and he leads our American operations.

We've launched a two-phase aftercare facility in Cambodia. We have a school and a reintegration project that works with the families. The girls in our home in Cambodia who have been sold into sex trafficking, as soon as they come into our home, we start working with their families back in the provinces. Our social workers work with them on why they were exploited in the first place. Some of it's because of poverty; some of it is because of lack of awareness. So we do social enterprise with them. I authorised a payment the other day for fifty chickens and a moped, so that after two years when one of the girls graduates through the school programme, her family will have a more stable environment to go back to. As of last year, we launched a new project, a stabilisation programme, that takes girls who have been rescued for the first eight weeks after their rescue. We take pretty much all trafficked children in Cambodia through that programme. It's amazing and we've launched it in several other countries.

What do you think we, as individuals here and as local churches, need to do in order to lean more into areas of worship and justice? How do we become better worshippers of God and better rescuers of men and women?

MS: I don't know whether I'm the authority on that but all I know is that, if you commit yourself to a local church, however long that's going to be, you're in, you're not a spectator of it. What happens is that, without really even realising it, every week you're in an atmosphere of worship. Your heart is reminded that God is alive. The fact that he is alive means that I can be alive and that my city could come alive. It means that there's hope for people, for my family, for the people who live down the street.

Church is God's genius plan for keeping us all in the right place. Out of that, when you worship your heart keeps soft. It's amazing how quickly our hearts can go cold – I'm telling you that from experience. It's amazing. Someone might say something hurtful to you, there might be a wound, a pain that hasn't healed – your church worship is the thing that keeps you soft. When your heart is soft, anything can happen. That's when God has you in the perfect place. When your heart is soft, you love people, you want to serve people, you want to give your money away, you want to give your life away to the calling of God, you want to run down the street and give £20 to someone you've never met before. You end up doing crazy stuff because God can use you. I don't understand all the other stuff that goes along with that, but all I know is that worship is so powerful. If there isn't that in your life, you're never going to make it. It's all completely cerebral and your heart doesn't engage. Always make sure, every day you're worshipping – singing, whistling, reading, listening to something in the car. Just something that keeps you soft.

BC: My pastor says that praise is the precursor to breakthrough. I think that if we're going to see this world change, worship and honouring God is one of the things that does do that. When we go through our trials and tribulations as the people of God, people are watching us. When we decide to declare and lift the name of Jesus with hymns, people see. What I see in these moments – and sometimes I find it difficult, when I've been in a brothel or met people in slavery – is how do you link it with this moment right now, when people are singing in worship? Sometimes I find it hard personally to go from different environments to say, 'God, where are you in this?' I realise that when I'm planted and rooted in worshipping God, it's what gives me the strength to see the breakthrough. I've seen the impossible being done because I've worshipped through it, praised through it, declared through it, trusted God through it. That's what worship is.

I love reading the book of Psalms. Sometimes we treat worship and praise as something we do when we feel like it. In the Psalms it doesn't say, 'I feel' like praising the Lord, it says *I will*. There's something about your will that you can harness and train. I think that's what Paul and Silas did – they probably didn't feel like praising the Lord, but they willed. Your will and your praise can see breakthrough.

How have you guys navigated through failure in your lives? Personally and in ministry? When you have tough times, one of the characteristics of our generation is that there is a huge temptation to quit when the going gets tough. How have you got through those times when you've felt like chucking in the towel or there's been a failure?

MS: Well, I think there are two sorts of failure. There's personal failure, where there's a tragedy maybe – perhaps there's been something in your life that's gone horribly wrong or deeply affected you and your family. That's one that is a deep sense of tragedy. Then there's the level of failure when someone's written a bad review about your record – 'Ah, I've failed.' So that's completely meaningless. There are different levels of that.

By the grace of God, I've experienced lots of failure on a peripheral level where I've invested my heart into lots of music and no one likes it or no one's bought it, the radio won't play it or no one turned up at shows. You can handle that sort of stuff because it doesn't really matter. I've lived an incredibly blessed life where I've married a wonderful woman and have an amazing family. If something happened close to home that would be mind-blowingly difficult. All the failures that happen around you – you can easily get over those if the core of your life is good. Does that make sense? Then you're not really worried about those other failures: as long as you feel like you're doing the right thing and your family is together, you can sort of get through anything.

BC: I think it's good to acknowledge that you will fail and that's OK. Sometimes I get really intense about failure because I really don't want to mess things up. But it will happen. Everyone fails. We need to take heart that even the best of us fail. But the important thing is to choose the keeping on, keeping on – it's about endurance.

Back in the early days of Hope for Justice, I made some mistakes that essentially meant I got a phone call to my office from someone who's involved in the industry that I fight against. They threatened me, 'Ben's children go to a great school, don't they?' Basically, it meant my wife, the children and I had to move out of my house. Those were dark days. I took on a lot of blame for that. I had to make a phone call to my wife; that was the worst phone call I have ever had to make in my life: 'Get the children from school.' That was all because I didn't put the right investment into security processes – I was a little bit too gung-ho at the start of Hope for Justice. It led to the worst few weeks of my life. I had to battle with that. I don't know what you would think if you put your family in danger like that. It was awful.

I had to remind myself who I was. I had to get out of bed. There are still times at Hope for Justice when I struggle to get out of bed. I find it hard. I don't find this an easy subject. Criticism – it destroys me. Certainly, when it came to my children's lives, it was overwhelming. I started to remind myself of who I was in God and kept on going. It was all through the power of prayer – praying for my family, praying for protection, starting to learn scriptures about who I was, how I was part of a Kingdom that will never be shaken. I kept on going. That's what defines someone. It's about longevity. It's why I honour Martin and the leaders who have gone before us. It's about perseverance.

It's great that you emphasise that family comes first, before ministry. How have you guys protected that and made sure that there is space in your lives? How have you made sure that those rhythms are there to persevere for the long haul?

BC: I haven't been great at it actually. For the first few years, I was so consumed by the vision that when I was at home I wasn't really at home. That's easy for us to do I suppose. I don't think it was until the last two years that I really got this.

I sat with a businessman who had started a well-known brand. He gave me some of the best advice I've ever been given. He said, 'Ben, here's how it goes with your family. Five, ten, fifteen, gone.' I thought, wow. I've got to invest more time with my children. When I'm at home, I need to be at home. It's been a real challenge for me. It's meant learning that Hope for Justice isn't Ben Cooley's mission; it's God's mission.

MS: I'd echo that. I think that it's about trying to have a long-term view as well. You've got twenty-four hours in the day. We're human beings. You can't do everything. I am learning to realise that God has called me to do this. He's in charge. He's got it.

For me in my world, obviously there's a commercial element to what I do – selling records, being on the road, earning a living. It's very easy for me to get caught up in thinking, 'I've got to do that tour because if I don't do that people will forget about me.' Or, 'There's another artist that's flying at the minute, I've got to be in there.' It's about being sure what God has called you to do. For me, I have to remind myself that God called me to sing over people. He didn't necessarily call me to sell records or go on tour or sing to loads of people. That isn't necessary to the calling – it's part of it but I've got to stick to the main thing.

For all creative people, it's very hard to balance being passionate about your art and being really into it; whatever the end product is, it needs an obsessive element to make it great. It needs you to be completely focused. But the problem is that's always at the expense of your relationships. In my case, it'll be my wife saying, 'You're home but you're not here' – I'll have a new song running through my brain. I think the creative thing is almost like having a mistress in your marriage. It's a very strange thing. You have to realise you don't have to have an affair, if you can understand that language. It's attractive, it's brilliant – but I can control it. I have to learn to control it, because I would like to still be married. And I would like to be friends with my children. I'd like to have a house full of people and do life and feed my soul and go and see a few football matches. I'm not going to sell my whole soul to this thing over here which is telling me it's going to validate my life.

The ironic thing that I've discovered is that if I submit my life to God – Psalm 24 says keep your hands clean and your heart pure, so if you try to do that, pursue God and put him first – then all these things seem to work out. When I got married, I thought I was never going to write another song again. I thought it was all going to disappear – I need space, I need time, I need to sit on a hill for three days and download from God. Actually, I feel like I started to write my best songs once I had children. My life was crazy, chaotic – we've got six children, it's mad. I remember the scripture, 'Seek first the Kingdom of God and all these things follow on.' I think I'm more creative now than I have ever been. That's in the context of school, homework, parents' evenings – it's mad. But within that madness, God is gracious.

YOU WANT TO KNOW WHAT THE HOLY SPIRIT IS DOING IN YOUR CITY? I CAN GUARANTEE YOU HE'S ENGAGING THOSE WHO ARE FAR FROM HIM.

Valuing what God values

Jay Pathak

Jay is the Lead Pastor of the Mile High Vineyard Church in Colorado, and co-wrote the book, *The Art of Neighboring* (Grand Rapids, Michigan: Baker Books, 2012), with Dave Runyon.

Things can happen to you at gatherings like the Cause to Live For which can change you permanently. God can speak to you; he can reveal calling and next steps, your assignment for him for this season. It's important that, after God does speak to you, you tell someone; you need to find someone you can be accountable to who can make sure that vision or direction God has given you comes to pass. It's easy to be on fire for God in that kind of environment, isn't it? But then sometimes, when we go back to normal life and reality sets in, there is the potential to lose some of that spark.

How do we make sure that we keep in step with the Holy Spirit? Also, how can we be sure to be doing things that we know God cares about when we are not surrounded by other believers and amazing worship?

See, when I first came to faith, it was through a legitimate encounter with God. I was reading the Bible and the presence of God filled my room. I began sobbing like a small girl – no, that's not fair to small girls. It was much worse than that. I definitely knew that God was real and he loved me – I just knew it. My instant reaction after this moment was to tell other people what had happened to me – and the only people I knew didn't know Jesus. So I started telling my friends. I had zero biblical knowledge or theology or apologetics – it was like, 'Man, this is so true, you should know Jesus.' They didn't even know what they thought about that stuff. I didn't have an answer to anything they were going to ask me besides: 'This is true and you should know Jesus.'

Do you know what's strange about that? It worked. People could see such a dramatic change in my life that they started to follow Jesus. I had friends around me following Jesus with me. It was almost by accident. We did (what I would later discover was called) Bible studies. I didn't know they were Bible studies; I wasn't sophisticated enough to know that. I would say, 'Let's get together and talk about this.'

I look back on those studies now and think most of what we were saying was pure heresy; we were making things up. But it was fresh and alive. We were responding to God. Over time, I ended up in a church – a great church. I started getting to know other people who loved God and followed Jesus. I started to experience more and more passion in my life with God. But, as I started to do this, something really strange happened. I got further away from people who didn't know Jesus. Not only was I further away from them, but something inside me changed. I was inspired by the spaces I was in with people who knew Jesus and the amount of excitement in the room, but something inside my heart began to grow cold.

Environments like the Cause to Live For almost became like Christian crack to me – like it was a drug; I needed the constant high of different spiritual environments where I would have encounters with God's presence. But it would never seem to remain and stick with me. The momentum of our lives as we follow Jesus, specifically when we're in church, unfortunately has a tendency to turn inwards. As we grow in our lives with God, if we're not paying attention, we will find ourselves more and more involved in Christian community. We then lose track of the world that is going on around us. I'm not saying Christian events that build up the Church are not great. I'm saying that there are things that God values more than great church experiences.

This truth is seen throughout the Scriptures; Jesus is really clear that God values those who do not know him more than those who do. Let that sink in for a second. You're thinking, 'That's heresy. You're still doing heresy!' He values those outside in a way that's disorienting for those of us who would see ourselves as inside. The truth is, if you want to know that you're keeping in step with the Holy Spirit, you need to love what God loves and be involved in what God is involved in. One of the ways you know that you can be a part of what God is doing is by being involved and engaged with the lost. Make your life and your passion and your purpose and your energy, your time and your prayers be about the lost.

As pastors, if we want churches that are healthy, and if we want to know that God's Spirit is with us, we should be about the lost. Jesus had this incredible knack for offending religious people. Whenever he encountered religious people, they would get angry with him. Eventually, that anger boiled over and they confronted him on a series of occasions about why he seems to love the wrong people so much. Why isn't he playing with the team he's supposed to be playing with? Why is he working with the people who are outside more than the people who are on the inside?

In Luke 15, he tells a series of stories which describe not only what he's doing but also why he's doing it and the way he's exemplifying God's heart through his life. Have a look at Luke 15, because there are some incredibly controversial things there, where Jesus challenges our preconceived notions and the kind of common momentum that we have if we follow our life with God. If we're not careful, if we're not thoughtful, we end up growing inwardly instead of engaging with those who are outside.

Listen to what Luke says: 'Tax collectors and other notorious sinners often came to listen to Jesus teach' (Luke 15.1 NLT). I like that – I like the 'notorious sinners' bit – not the normal sinners, the *notorious* ones. 'This made the Pharisees and the teachers of the religious law complain that he was associating with such sinful people, even eating with them.' What would it be like if we had such an incredible ministry, like Jesus, that religious people look on and say, 'Why do you love those who are so far away?' You need space and time to be with those who are lost and hurting. Wouldn't it be great? When was the last time a religious person confronted you about loving those who are so far away? I'd love that.

Jesus tells many stories in the Bible that show just how important it is to him to love the lost.

> Suppose one of you has a hundred sheep and loses one of them. Doesn't he leave the ninety-nine in the open country and go after the lost sheep until he finds it? And when he finds it, he joyfully puts it on his shoulders and goes home. Then he calls his friends and neighbours together and says, 'Rejoice with me; I have found my lost sheep.' I tell you that in the same way there will be more rejoicing in heaven over one sinner who repents than over ninety-nine righteous people who do not need to repent.
>
> (Luke 15.4–7)

I want to make sure that you understand what he said: there's more joy in heaven over the one who's far away that comes, than the ninety-nine he already had. Can you imagine the Pharisees, the good religious people, listening to this answer and thinking, 'What? That's rude! That is not nice!' And he says, 'Well, that's the truth.'

Then there's more!

> Or suppose a woman has ten silver coins and loses one. Doesn't she light a lamp, sweep the house and search carefully until she finds it? And when she finds it, she calls her friends and neighbours together and says, 'Rejoice with me; I have found my lost coin.' In the same way, I tell you, there is rejoicing in the presence of the angels of God over one sinner who repents.
>
> (Luke 15.8–10)

Let me give you a little cultural context here to show you why this story is so significant, specifically for single women. In the culture at that time, wearing ten coins effectively showed that your family was wealthy. Unmarried women would wear these as a way of showing that not only were they wealthy, but available: 'This could be yours, oh . . . and the coins!' With all the single women wearing ten, what woman would walk out wearing nine? Instead, you'd be tearing up the room trying to find that tenth coin!

If you think about this passage, it doesn't take long to see it's all about the lost. In our culture today, to be called 'lost' is offensive. If I say 'I'm found and you're lost,' that's offensive, right? But that's not how Jesus sees the lost here. Lostness in the passage denotes value. The lostness of the sheep and the coin shows how valuable those items are.

For example, when my wife Danielle and I were engaged we had no money. I had spent all the money I had buying an engagement ring. Only a month or so before the wedding, she turns to me and says, 'I have to tell you something. I can't find the ring. I don't know where it is.'

I said, 'I'm sorry, what? Where did you look?'

She starts crying and I tell her, 'We're going to find the ring, it's OK.'

So we start in all the normal places: the kitchen sink, the bathroom, by the bed. By the end of that day, I'm on my hands and knees, putting my fingers where the carpet reaches the wall, pulling back the carpet, searching with my fingertips – as if the ring would fly off and get jammed into the wall somehow. It showed how desperate I was! We had taken apart every sink in the house, just in case it had been dropped down a plughole and she could not remember where it went. That is how desperate it was: 'Until this is found, we're not doing anything else – because I don't have any more money. So we are going to find the ring. Cancel your plans; we're going to find the ring. Focus.'

Value. Purpose. Jesus is saying, 'This is how I see those who do not know me. It all stops. It all stops, until we pull them in. All this other religious stuff we do, if it isn't to that end, if it isn't to reach and engage and draw, to show them how valuable they are, then you don't understand.' The Pharisees were concentrating on their foundness. But Jesus is saying, you are always found so that you might pursue those who are lost because they are so valuable to the Father. What Jesus is really saying is, 'Do you not hear my heart? Catch my heart.'

Of course, Jesus then goes on to tell the story of the lost son. What a powerful story! You've probably heard it before – commonly called the Parable of the Prodigal Son. It's about a younger son who is tired of his dad, and affectedly says, 'Hey Dad, I know I'm going to get my inheritance some day but I would prefer not to wait until you're dead. Is there any way we could pretend you're dead now and I could get that money?' In other words, he is saying, 'I wish you were dead, give me the money.' I don't think you need to be a parent to think about what you would do in a scenario like that. If my son or daughter said, 'I wish you were dead, can I have the money?' I would say, 'Nobody gets to talk to me like that. Go to your room.'

What's so amazing about this story is that the father gives him the inheritance. He just says, 'OK.' He has to know that the son is going to go crazy and of course, he does, going off to a distant land and basically living out a hip-hop video, we all know the sort! Then eventually the money runs out and as soon as that happens, as with so many people living crazy lives, all the friends who were there for the good times leave. Then something happens that the son was not expecting: a famine sweeps through the land. That's always what happens to prodigals that run away and think they can have as much fun as they want. They eventually find that the fun runs out and a famine sets in.

That's what happens to the lost son. In the midst of the famine, with all the money spent, the son finds himself feeding the pigs. While he is looking at the pig food he thinks, 'Man, that pig food looks good, I should probably eat some of that.' That's when, Luke states, 'he came to his senses' (Luke 15.17). These are interesting words because Jesus is describing that we can go through all kinds of stupid decisions, but there's a moment, quite literally a miracle, often in our lives, where we go, 'Wait a minute, what am I doing?' What's weird about this story is that he didn't come to his senses in the middle of the hip-hop video. Why didn't he come to his senses when the money ran out, his friends left, or when he started working with pigs? No, there's something magical about the pig food. I don't know what it was and nor do you – no one knows!

Seriously, in the bit of time I've done pastoral stuff in churches, I've seen that this is the miracle of how people's lives change. You never know what it's going to take for somebody to come to their senses. Sometimes people come to their senses because of the smallest things. Someone once came up to me and said, 'I need to talk to you. I need an appointment.' We took a seat and immediately he broke down in tears. I asked what happened. He explained how he was with his girlfriend and they were kissing and lying on each other. I continued to ask what happened. But that was all.

He said, 'This is when I realised I could feel the lust pulling in my heart, ready to pull me off a cliff. I knew if I didn't draw a line right here, I could open up something I would regret later.'

I looked at him and thought, that seems to be the conviction of the Holy Spirit. I said, 'You're responding to God's conviction,' and we prayed together. I thought it was amazing.

The same day, not much later, I had another appointment. A young man came in and sat down. He said that his girlfriend had told him to come to talk to me. I asked him what was going on. He said that they'd been struggling; they'd crossed some boundaries – lines they knew God wouldn't want them to cross but they crossed them anyway. I asked what the lines were. He said they'd fallen.

Have you ever played that game? Can you see how he avoided saying *anything* of substance up to this point? He went on to say that what he and his girlfriend were doing was not a big deal. After I pressed him further, he told me they were regularly having sex. He then said, 'I know God isn't really thrilled about it – whatever, what're you going to do, right?'

I thought, 'How about not having sex?'

What was so weird was to see those two appointments almost back to back. What makes one person feel convicted about one thing and the other person feel unconcerned? I have no idea. Here's what I do know: when you come to your senses, you'd better respond. If you harden your heart instead, you have no idea how long it's going to take until you come to your senses again. There have been moments in my life, when I've come to my senses, when the Holy Spirit was working in me and I brushed it off. I can tell you moments in my life where it took years before I woke up to that. I look back and think, there are other times when God was trying to talk to me about something and I ignored it. I was afraid and I thought my way was better. What's it going to take? That's what you have to ask yourself. If you don't want to respond to the conviction of the Holy Spirit right now, do you want it to get a lot worse before you respond? The reason God convicts us is because he loves us and he wants to change things.

So the son eventually comes to his senses and heads back. He prepares his speech: 'Father, I have sinned against heaven and against you. I am no longer worthy to be called your son; make me like one of your hired servants' (Luke 15.18–19). I don't know if you've ever made a speech, for school or something: 'It was the dog. Some water fell on my homework and then the dog ate it.' That's not believable. Let's try again, just: 'The dog ate it.' That doesn't work. So you practise what you're going to say. You practise the speech. So, as the son is walking home, he is practising the speech. Of course, you know the story: the father comes rushing out and runs towards him. Imagine you're the son. You look up and there's the father, running towards you. 'Huh, I wonder why he's running. Never really seen him run before.'

I don't know what you would think but my thought would be: when he gets closer, I'm going to duck because I know he's going to hit me. That would be my natural assumption. Instead, the father wraps his arms around him. The son still gives his stupid speech: 'Father, I have sinned against heaven and against you . . .' But the father interrupts the speech at this point. 'Enough of that – let's throw a party. My son who was dead is now alive.'

Even after he has been hugged, the son continues his speech. Even after he has been loved, the son continues to explain. What in the world is wrong with that boy? You know what's wrong with him? The same things that are wrong with us. Ultimately, we live with a deep-seated fear that we're always going to be in trouble. That when we're with God, when we come close to him, we're going to be in trouble. Jesus paints this picture so clearly: he says, when the lost come in, you can be with the Father and embrace this moment.

Of course, there is an older son who doesn't participate in the party, have you noticed that? This is when Jesus is really turning the screws on the Pharisees. He's effectively saying, 'You're like the older son who won't come into the party because you're mad at the younger son: the one who has blown it and messed it up; that son is being embraced – and you see that as unfair. You're right, it's not fair. But here's the difference: do you want to join the party or stand outside whining about it? There's a party and you're welcome to be a part of it – you can be a part of watching what God wants to do in bringing lost people home.' That's what you can do; that's how you join the party. If we want a clear sense that the Holy Spirit is with us, working in our churches, we need to be about seeing the lost come home. That's what the Holy Spirit is up to. That's what he's up to all over the world right now.

Imagine that we're on a camping trip. It's a dark, cool night and we're sitting by the campfire. I stand up and say, 'Listen everyone, I need your attention. My daughter has been lost. I don't know where she is. She's eight years old. The last time I saw her she was wearing a pink jacket. She's about this tall.' I circulate a picture and then I continue: 'If we break up right now and hurry, we can catch her up. The last time I saw her, she was walking that way. Please can you help me? I don't know where she went.' I grab a few people and run off into the woods.

Some people gather round and say, 'Before we go and look, we need to have a great plan. I heard there are books written about finding people who are lost in situations like this.'

Someone else says, 'No, we should sing. I once sang a song about being lost in the woods. It might help us. What do you say? Let's sing it!'

The campers sing the song about helping the lost people around the campfire and, before you know it, they have some marshmallows out; they're toasting them over the fire. Then if I, the father of the missing girl, come back from the woods, to that campfire, to see people sitting around singing and toasting marshmallows, I would walk away. It would be evident from the other people's behaviour that they don't understand my heart, who I am, and they don't value what I value. Walking away would be the best you could hope for from a desperate father. The worst is . . . much, much worse.

Jesus is saying to the Pharisees (and to us), if you want to stay fresh in your life with God, join him with the search party. Go and rescue those who are far. They're lost and don't know it. They're not choosing to be lost, they just don't know it. Have you ever been lost and didn't know it? You never think you're lost; you try to find your way. Most people don't know they're lost – but they are. God says come and join me in the search party, feel my heart, come and be with me.

You want to know what the Holy Spirit is doing in your city? I can guarantee you one thing for sure: he's engaging those who are far from him. There is someone in your city now, likely not very far from you, who is at this moment asking, 'God, are you real? I don't know if you're real.' There'll be somebody who is in a difficult marriage saying, 'God, is there any way you can help?' There are people all over your city that God is drawing by his Spirit. My personal experience is that a dangerous prayer to pray is 'God give me your heart for people, for this city.' It is dangerous because God will answer it. You begin to break, you feel what he feels. You can't do business as usual. You can't go back and do church stuff – not in the same way, anyway. Church has to prepare and equip us for what God's heart is about: being part of the search party, pushing out into the darkness, grabbing hold of those who are far from him and joining in the wonderful experience of a life with Jesus.

WE HAVE TO DEAL
WITH FEAR IN ORDER
TO WALK AND GO
FORWARD IN THE FAITH
THAT GOD HAS FOR US.

Fear or faith?

Jay Pathak

I have an incredible capacity to be encouraged and discouraged. In the span of one week, I can feel really excited about something and then very discouraged and depressed – in one week! Do you ever experience this in your life? Has it ever happened to you in one day or one hour or one minute? It's happened to me within a minute. And it was in this minute that God began to change something within me.

I've had an incredible opportunity over this past year. I'm a pastor in Denver, Colorado. In short, my family and I were part of an initiative that took place within a series of churches; we ended up with just short of seventy churches involved across many denominations. Over the space of three weeks, we preached the same sermons about how God wants us to love our neighbours.

A friend and I wrote these sermons in conjunction with the mayor's office – we even put videos online describing what we were doing. It was a really exciting initiative to be part of – tens of thousands of people heard the same sermons over three weeks in our city. Isn't that pretty cool? During the final week of this initiative, we threw a huge party to celebrate good neighbours and being part of our neighbourhoods. The mayor of our city came to our church service for this party. It was really fun. It was also a little nerve-wracking with the mayor sitting there, looking at me.

I preached. I preached my guts out. I preached about what I thought God could do in our city and how he could see people drawn into a relationship with him. How the city would know that God is alive. I was passionate; I was shouting; I was whispering. Even a tear or two came to my eye. Afterwards, a powerful politician came up to me and said, 'Jay! That was incredible. What you did – that was amazing! Sitting in your church, listening to you preach – that was amazing!'

I replied, 'Thank you, I'm so encouraged.' And I did feel very encouraged as I looked at him and the party and thought about the city.

Then he said, 'Maybe you should use that speaking gift for something that would be more effective.'

I said, 'What? I'm sorry, I missed that.'

He said, 'Listen, I'm not trying to be a jerk but you're a good communicator. Most pastors are just "blah, blah, blah", saying random stuff that helps people feel better for a little bit. But I think you could actually do something. Have you ever considered politics?'

'Wow!' I thought, but I said, 'No, no. I've never considered politics.' At the back of my mind, I was making a mental note to consider politics.

He said, 'You know, this was great but, at most, how many folks will hear you? There are what – six, maybe eight hundred people here at your services. That's not very many people. What would it look like for you to speak to and influence thousands, tens of thousands, whole cities? You know you could do that as a politician, right? What are eight hundred people going to do? Nothing, not much. But you could affect tens of thousands as a politician, as a communicator.'

A minute before, I'd thought 800 was a lot. It felt pretty good actually – a minute before.

He continued, 'Even in this network, this initiative, you've preached to tens of thousands of people. But our city has a population of a quarter of a million. The Denver metro area has two and a half million people. That means, best-case scenario, you're not going to affect two point five million people – no matter what – with whatever it is you think you're doing. But you're definitely going to affect a nation as a politician. You can change policies in a city and affect a nation.'

The more he said, the more I thought, 'Politics sounds pretty good, now that you mention it.'

The politician's comment had really rattled me. In the space of a minute, I went from feeling very encouraged to really depressed, and from thinking the initiative with the churches in our city was going to change a huge amount to believing it might change nothing at all. I felt as if I were wasting my life. I went home and I put on the film *300*. Watching films often helps me to think things through and work them out.

Based on true events that took place in 480 BC, *300* is about a war between the Persian Empire and the Greek city states. In the film, as the Persians advance through the known world, various nations and states sign treaties, effectively handing over their power. But there's one Greek city state – Sparta – that defies the Persians. The Spartans say, 'No, we're not going to let you do this, we're not going to give in to fear. We're fighting back.' Nevertheless, some factions within Sparta will not allow the state to go to war. So the king, Leonidas, gathers his personal guard of only 300 men and goes to fight the huge Persian army of hundreds of thousands. The 300 Spartans stand their ground at a narrow pass that is the entrance to Greece, a place called the 'Hot Gates' in the film. Because the pass is so narrow – too narrow for the huge Persian army to fight in effectively – the Spartans keep at bay and kill tens of thousands before they themselves are killed.

It's a cool story, although you might think that 300 people lost their lives for nothing – they merely delayed the inevitable and then they died. But that wasn't the end of the story. The Spartans' sacrifice awakened the rest of the Greek city states: the example set by those 300 men helped them to see that they too could find the strength to stand up to the Persians. After all, if 300 warriors could inflict that kind of damage, then the rest of them should fight and not surrender.

The truth is that change happens in cities and in nations and in the Church of Jesus Christ because a few stand against fear. Those few create a ripple effect throughout the world that says, 'We should not be afraid.' However, in the Church and in my own heart there is a very real battle with fear. What that politician did was to trigger the fear that I would be insignificant, useless or nothing.

As I watched *300*, I believe God was reminding me that if my faith could awaken only a few, it would be worth it. What if 300 or 600 said that they would not allow fear to dominate their lives? What if they lived as though God were actually alive? And as if his Kingdom was the most valuable thing in the world? That the life he offers is more precious than anything else that could be offered? What if we actually lived as if we were in the middle of the only story that really counts? Is it possible that if they did – if *we* did – then many others would be awakened to live a life they never dreamt possible, because just a few live with courage?

Fear stands between you and the destiny God has for you. Fear: it's subtle; it's sneaky. It's amazing how it creeps into the fabric of who we are. It takes on different forms in a way we can't even recognise. We live in a world that is so drenched in fear that it's hard even to see it. From the adverts we watch on TV to the stories we read in newspapers, much of our society will play on our fears about being inadequate or uninteresting. Our culture tells us, 'Buy a fast car to make you more attractive' or 'Go on a gap year to the Galapagos to become a more exciting person.'

Car commercials and concerns about retirement and finance tug at us and make us worry. They make us wonder if we're significant enough or interesting enough or secure enough. Unless we deal with fear purposefully or directly, we actually prevent ourselves from hearing from God. We're disabled because we're so clogged up with the small things that consume us, we can't hear about the great adventure we're being called to.

The truth is that we have to deal with fear in order to move forward in the faith that God has for us. The Bible tells us so. In the book of Revelation, the people who are thrown into the lake of fire, after murderers and idolaters, are cowards. Cowards. God hates the fact that fear dominates us. He wants us to be free. We also see this in Numbers, chapter 13.

Numbers 13 is the story of how God's people came right up to the edge of the land he had promised them. They sent some spies into the land; the spies brought back a report about it. This is the account they gave to Moses:

> We went into the land to which you sent us, and it does flow with milk and honey! Here is its fruit. But the people who live there are powerful, and the cities are fortified and very large. We even saw descendants of Anak there. The Amalekites live in the Negev; the Hittites, Jebusites and Amorites live in the hill country; and the Canaanites live near the sea and along the Jordan.
>
> (Numbers 13.27–29)

Effectively, what they said was the land was full of people – scary people. One of the spies, Caleb, sensed what was happening: he 'silenced the people before Moses and said, "We should go up and take possession of the land, for we can certainly do it'" (Numbers 13.30). Basically, he said, 'Stop talking! Stop freaking everybody out. This is our land and we're meant to go and take it. Shh! Quiet.' But that didn't work . . .

> But the men who had gone up with him said, 'We can't attack those people; they are stronger than we are.' And they spread among the Israelites a bad report about the land they had explored. They said, 'The land we explored devours those living in it. All the people we saw there are of great size. We saw the Nephilim there (the descendants of Anak come from the Nephilim). We seemed like grasshoppers in our own eyes, and we looked the same to them.'
>
> (Numbers 13.31–33)

It's a fascinating story and it gives you an idea of how fear can take hold. Fear does two really strange things. First, fear maximises obstacles; it makes them larger than they actually are. The Israelite spies go from saying that there are a few big people in the land to saying that *all* the inhabitants are giants. Second, fear makes us assume that others see us a certain way, which can change our perceptions for the worse. The Israelite spies say that they felt like grasshoppers and they believed that the people in the land saw them that way, too.

It's important to think about who the Israelites were. They were people who had seen miracle after miracle. They were slaves who were set free and saw God cause plagues. They saw pillars of cloud and fire, seas parting and crashing back, and water coming out of rocks. They'd seen incredible things – yet they reached the very edge of their destiny and fear threatened to keep them from it.

If you know the story, you know that all the people believe the bad report and God says, 'Never mind. I guess you're not going in.' Then for forty years, they do laps of the desert until all the people over a certain age are dead, except for Joshua and Caleb – simply because they surrendered to fear. Isn't that a crazy thought?

Fear works the same way in your mind. Whatever it is God is asking you to do right now, your first battle is against fear – the fear that makes the obstacles in front of you seem huge. The hardest challenge on your journey will be whatever is right in front of you. It's only by looking back that we realise our fears are stupid. When you revisit things you were afraid of years before, don't you often wonder why you were afraid? You think, 'What was wrong with me? God had been so faithful to me, why was I afraid to take the next step? It seemed like such a big deal. But once I did it, I realised that God was with me – of course it was going to work!' Have you ever thought that? I'm sure you have.

I often think back to when I first surrendered my life to Jesus. God was pursuing me; I had a sense that God was real but I thought that following him was too much to ask. I didn't know if I should do so. I wasn't sure if I wanted to become like *them* – Christians. I was nervous. I felt there was a lot of risk involved. When I look back now, I think, 'What exactly was I risking? Things like hanging out with my high school buddies getting drunk? Wow, big sacrifice. What was I thinking? Why did that seem like such a big deal?' It's because it was the challenge that was in front of me.

I remember I went on to lead a small group. I thought it would be difficult; I thought I was going to blow it. I remember being terrified. The guy who was leading the small group that I was already in helped me to start it. He announced to the group one day, 'Jay is going to lead the next small group.' Everyone thought it was a great idea. Later, I started to invite people to my small group but they would say, 'No, no . . .'

I went to my girlfriend – who is now my wife – and I said, 'Are you coming to my small group?'

She said, 'No, I don't think so.'

With her refusal to join, too, I didn't think I could lead a group. But I reminded myself that God was telling me to do this, and, of course, God met me in it.

I remember the first time I preached. I thought it was such a big deal – I thought I would be terrible. And my preaching was terrible. But I did it and God was in it. He was faithful. I remember thinking about being called to plant a church. It was so clear that I had been called to do so. I remember thinking, 'Oh no, this is crazy, I can't do this. The other place where I am is so much better. This is perfect, right where I'm at. I can't take that next step!' Of course, eventually, I overcame my fear. I could tell you about other things that I'm afraid of, that I think are a really big deal. But they aren't; I'm making them bigger than they are.

There may be things in your life that you avoid or make excuses not to do. Perhaps the obstacles aren't nearly as big as you think they are. It's simply a matter of taking the next step – a step of faith to overcome that obstacle. It's realising that it's about actively pursuing a life with God which will enable you to become the person you are supposed to be. You might be right on the edge of a destiny that God has set up for you and all you need do is say 'yes'.

This can happen in many different ways. For example, feeling angry about an issue might mean that you're being called to do something about it. Often, instead of taking action and pursuing a calling revealed by anger, people blog cynically about it. Cynicism can be a mass form of fear and cowardice. It's much easier to criticise other people's steps of courage than it is to live out our own.

Ultimately, what's amazing about the story in Numbers 13 to me is how the people became more comfortable in the desert, in the middle of nowhere, than with obtaining the incredible thing that God offered them. I think back on different times in my life and how I managed to live with some things that were worth nothing and useless. The reason I lived with them for so long was because I was used to them.

Risk and faith challenge fears that are often rooted in a desire for security and comfort. We love to feel comfortable. We have so many little comforts. If you want to test this, notice what happens when the internet is down for five minutes; the wireless doesn't work and you immediately think, 'This is awful, this is morally offensive, this is wrong, I deserve – I am owed – wireless.' For me, fast food always reveals how comfortable I am. If I'm at McDonald's and the person serving me has the audacity to say, 'Can you step aside and I'll get you your fries – it's taking a little bit of time,' my response will be: 'This is crazy. Really, *really*? You're going to give me this for free, right? This is crazy, my food is meant to instantly appear.' Think of how ridiculous that attitude is; it's a mindset that arises out of being so secure and comfortable. God cuts 180 degrees against that.

For you to respond to God, your comfort and security will most certainly be threatened. You will have to move from the familiar and safe; you'll have to stop worrying so much about what people think about you and possibly losing the comfort of the friends who appreciate your quirkiness. If you take the risk, it will change you and it will change your family. There are some of us who are afraid of how other people will perceive us. It's easier to keep managing their expectations than it is to step into what God is making clear to us. That is fear – a subtle form of fear.

Perhaps your fears centre on retirement. You think, 'Will I have enough money? How will I retire?' But, sadly, it may be that, because of the current economic situation, many of us may not be able to retire. But comfort doesn't equal happiness. That's a lie. Security does not equal joy. If we don't learn as a generation how to trust in God, we will be severely depressed. We have to learn how to trust God for our money, and not just believe that things will be different. God presses on those places of fear, security and comfort when he calls us to do something.

Often when we're called to do something, a far more secure, attractive and easy alternative will present itself to keep us from pursuing the calling. I've come to believe this so much that I've named it the 'Attractive Alternative Phenomenon'. It's the way God tests calling in our lives. I've seen this in my life whenever I've had to take a risk to follow my calling. There are times when I let an attractive alternative grab my attention, instead of focusing on everything God had planned for me. On those occasions when I didn't let the alternative seduce me, it changed everything. So, ironically, the attractive alternative is a positive sign for me now. When one pops up, I know that a calling is from God and that it will require sacrifice.

When I was helping to plant our church, I wondered whether I should become a full-time paid member of the church staff. However, at the time, I was working in sales and making a lot more money than I would have done working for the church, so I hesitated. Then God spoke so clearly.

My wife Danielle and I were driving to a conference, where I was to give a talk. I said to Danielle, 'God has got to speak, if he really wants me to leave this job. It would be a major sacrifice for us, financially – he's got to speak to us.'

'Well,' she said, 'if he speaks, we have to obey.'

I said, 'Definitely.'

We arrived and walked into the lobby of the conference venue and headed to the reception desk. There was someone checking in; he looked over at me and said, 'God's calling you to make a sacrifice. Give it all for him. Pastor the church.'

So I got home and weighed up what the man said – it's always wise to test prophecy against the Bible – but I knew that God had spoken. The next day, I walked into my boss's office and said to her: 'Here's the deal. You know I'm helping to plant a church. I believe God has called me to do that. It's time for me to resign. I want to honour this job and do it well; I can stay for two weeks, four weeks, whatever you need. I want to finish well for you.'

My boss said, 'Really? Are you sure you need to resign?'

I said, 'I really do. I've got to do this next thing.'

She told me to talk to the other managers to figure out how this was going to work.

A little while later, the director of the whole company came to my office. He sat down and said, 'Listen, I've heard from your manager that you've resigned. That's too bad.'

I said, 'It's just one of those things. I want to make sure I end well with you.'

He said, 'Great but, here's the thing. I'm probably going to have to hire two people to do what you do, initially, for sure. What I would like is for you to be here to train them to be effective.'

I said, 'Well, do you think four weeks would be enough?'

He said, 'No, no, no, it'll take like six months or so. Before you say no, we'll pay you double – for those six months.'

I was stunned. I was going to have to take a huge pay cut to plant the church. If the church didn't grow, we'd run out of money in about six months. The director told me to call my wife and think about it. So I called Danielle: 'You're not going to believe it. God has provided. All it's going to take is another six months – what's another six months, right? We'll get double pay and that sets us up for another number of months. So we'll be able to do all of this.'

'So . . .', she replied. I took a breath. She continued, 'That's all really exciting. But, here's the thing, did God speak or not?'

I knew she was right. I went to see the director. I said, 'Hey, listen. I'm going to turn down your offer. I'm sorry.'

He wasn't deterred. He said, 'I know your family lives back in Ohio. We're about to open a new branch there. I could give you some airline vouchers, travel things – how about you take a vacation – take a month off in the middle, full pay, it'll be fine.'

I laughed out loud. 'No, no, no. The answer's no. I don't have to think about this, the answer is no.'

There was a guy I had been sharing my faith with all the time I worked at the company. He said to me, 'God spoke to you, didn't he?'

I replied, 'Yeah, he did. I can't compete with that – I mean, I tried but I can't.'

I drove home that night thinking, 'What am I doing? This is so foolish.' And, superficially, it was foolish, financially speaking. But my choice wasn't about six months' pay – it was about obedience.

Obedience is about saying yes to something that God is asking, without even knowing what will happen next. Of course, I'd love to say, 'That's when the glory fell on me and started piling up inside my house. See, the Lord has provided all things.' It was the exact opposite. After six months, we had almost run out of money. I nearly phoned my old workplace to beg for my job back but, of course, God provided. He made a way. And if he hadn't, it wouldn't have mattered because I was concerned more with what God wanted. Obedience is not about you or about me; it's about how we respond to God and who we become in the process.

Fear also challenges us to negotiate. But we don't negotiate with God. When God asks a thing of you, you simply obey. I love negotiating – I negotiate all the time. I love saying things like, 'If I do that, what's going to happen? What exactly is that going to cost me in the end? How much should I write the cheque for?'

God says, 'Just sign the cheque; I'll fill in the cost for you. Choose to be a person who obeys in all the places of your life and I will tell you what it costs. I'll tell you as you go.'

We all know that this kind of courage is what we're meant to live for. You and I were meant to live brave, courageous lives of sacrifice. We know in our hearts that we were meant to live for something more. We were meant to be part of a story that's larger than our own little stories.

In the Kingdom death – sacrifice – brings life. What we know is that all we see and all we are will one day, not long from now, feel like a strange dream. If the story that we're a part of is true at all, we can be confident that God is reconciling all things to himself, and that one day everything will be made right. All pain, all suffering, all worry and all fear will be swallowed up by the power of his resurrection, as God redeems all flesh and all creation (see Colossians 1.20).

One day, those idle moments – when we held little negotiations with God to decide whether we would really trust him fully or not – will all seem so silly in light of his glory, his power and his majesty. The things we feared will seem so small in comparison to the vastness and the beauty of his Kingdom.

If God is asking you to give something up – even before you know what he's going to ask of you – pray: 'God, I choose to obey. If anything is in the way and keeps me from obeying you, I give you permission to remove it, to deal with it violently. Do whatever you need to help me to be obedient to you. Whatever stands in my way, deal with it. Change it, move it, destroy it. Do whatever needs to be done, that I might fully obey and that your life may be fully lived in me.'

That's one of those prayers which we can be pretty sure God will answer. I encourage you to be brave. When you say that prayer and mean it, I believe that God by his Spirit will draw near and take fear right out of your heart and fill you with a new, confident faith to live a life that you never imagined possible.

IN LIGHT OF ALL YOU'VE
DONE FOR ME, I LAY MY
LIFE DOWN AT YOUR
FEET.

'I Am Yours': the story behind the song

Dave Miller

Dave is the Worship Pastor at Trent Vineyard in Nottingham. He has written a number of songs and appeared on various Vineyard Worship recordings.

A few years ago, I wrote a song that we sang at the Cause to Live For conference called 'I Am Yours'. It is essentially a song of surrender to Jesus and to the purposes of God. It's a prayer of commitment to his Kingdom and his Cause – whatever the implications for us. John Wimber used to say, we are just 'change in his pocket, he can spend [us] as he wants'.[1] That heart posture is exactly what I wanted to capture and articulate in this song: 'I am yours, use me, Lord, as you please, as you please.' Here are the lyrics:

> At the cross, I humbly fall,
> To my knees, to my knees.
> I am yours, use me, Lord,
> As you please, as you please.
> I'd do anything, I'd go anywhere for you,
> Jesus, Saviour.

In light of all you've done for me,
I lay my life down at your feet.
What rights I have, I sacrifice
To you, my Lord, to you, oh Lord.
For you have bought me, at a price;
Now I am yours, wholly yours.
Use me, send me, I'm yours, completely;
All I have, I'm laying down before you.
Here I am, use me for your glory,
King Jesus, you're worth it all.

Whether it's this song specifically, or a different one that articulates the same sort of thing, I do believe this is a prayer that we need to be praying because it's about the sort of people we need to become – the sort of 'people' that God has called us to be and the sort of people that the world needs us to be.

The song grew in the soil of reflections around a well-known verse in Romans 12: 'Therefore, I urge you, brothers and sisters, in view of God's mercy, to offer your bodies as a living sacrifice, holy and pleasing to God – this is your true and proper worship' (Romans 12.1). Because this verse is quoted so often, we can easily miss its importance: this is actually a key moment in Paul's letter to the Church in Rome. Everything in the letter before this point focuses on theology, on doctrine, on what God has done. Everything after this point focuses on praxis, on doing, on how we should live. This verse is the turning point from one focus to the other. However, rather than it being a letter with two halves, two focuses, the beauty of this verse is that with it Paul grounds the one focus in the other, the latter in the former. The 'doing' is actually *grounded* in the 'knowing', the 'praxis' is *grounded* in the 'theology'. The verse divides neatly into two sections – one looks back to the previous chapters and one looks forward towards the chapters to come.

THEREFORE, I URGE YOU, BROTHERS AND SISTERS, IN VIEW OF GOD'S MERCY (ROMANS 12.1A)

Before Paul articulates what it is that he wants his readers to do, and before he clarifies what it is that he is 'urging' his brothers and sisters towards – namely offering their bodies as living sacrifices – he first gives the reason or motivation for it. The two terms ('therefore' and 'in view of God's mercy') are of central importance.

The word 'therefore' suggests that the requirement he is about to make is connected to and because of something that he has already said; it's a linking word, linking one idea to another. The phrase, 'in view of God's mercy', then helps to clarify what Paul is referring to when he uses 'therefore'. Whatever the 'therefore' is 'there for', it must have something to do with the 'mercy of God'. It's as if Paul is saying, 'Therefore, given everything I have just been saying about the mercies of God . . .' It functions as Paul's own summary of what he has been talking about. So, what has he said about the mercy of God?

To answer that we have to look at the whole first half of the letter. Because this verse is the key moment of transition in Romans, it suggests that Paul has more in view than just the previous paragraph. When Paul says 'therefore' in this verse, he is drawing not only the immediate literary context into view but also the previous 11 chapters – everything that he has previously said. I love the fact that a cursory glance through chapters 1—11 shows Paul developing this panoramic view of the height, breadth, width, beauty and majesty of God's mercy.

In Romans 1, we have the God who created us for himself and yet we rejected him and worshipped other things. In verse 21 Paul famously writes about humanity that, 'although they knew God, they neither glorified him as God nor gave thanks to him . . .' (Romans 1.21). In chapter 2, it's clear that it isn't only the Jewish nation who sinned in this way but that all humanity is accountable and God is the great judge before whom the whole of humanity is falling short. In chapter 3 it gets even bleaker: 'There is no one righteous, not even one' (Romans 3.10), writes Paul. But then we get to verse 21, and two words that the famous Welsh preacher, Martin Lloyd Jones, called the two most wonderful words, the two most vital words, in the Bible.[2] When everything seemed hopeless, humanity lost to sin, alienated from God, dead and without any capacity to restore things or make things right, Paul writes, 'but now'. And with those two words, hope enters the universe:

> But now apart from the law the righteousness of God has been made known, to which the Law and the Prophets testify. This righteousness is given through faith in Jesus Christ to all who believe.
>
> (Romans 3.21–22)

The mercy of God bursts through, in the bleak, dark, hopelessness of our sin: God sends Jesus, who dies on the cross in our place, for our sins, and it is through faith in him that we can now be reconciled to God – all is not lost! In Romans 4, Paul shows how it's not about earning salvation or belonging to the right group but through faith in Jesus that we are made right with God. When all seemed hopeless, God made a way; where we couldn't, he did, and he reconciled us to himself. In chapter 5, we now have peace with God because of Jesus, with the famous passage: 'But God demonstrates his own love for us in this: while we were still sinners, Christ died for us' (Romans 5.8). It's amazingly good news about the kindness and generosity of God, who has justified us freely by his grace (5.9), reconciled us to God (5.11) and reversed the consequences of Adam's sin in Genesis (5.12–20).

In chapter 6, Paul shows how we are now free from the power and slavery of sin that leads to death, and instead we are those who love righteousness which leads to eternal life. He writes, 'But now that you have been set free from sin and have become slaves of God, the benefit you reap leads to holiness, and the result is eternal life. For the wages of sin is death, but the gift of God is eternal life in Christ Jesus our Lord' (Romans 6.22–23). In chapter 7 we are free from law and dead to sin. We still wrestle with it; however, we do so now with the Holy Spirit's help. In Romans 8, Paul starts with this wonderful verse: 'Therefore, there is now no condemnation for those who are in Christ Jesus, because through Christ Jesus the law of the Spirit who gives life has set you free from the law of sin and death' (8.1–2). He goes on to show that the Holy Spirit is living in us, changing us, giving us new life. The Spirit makes us children of God, heirs with Christ. Through his kindness, we have been adopted into God's family; the same God who will, one day, make all things new, including creation itself! He goes on to say how we are chosen, called and predestined, how we are being continually changed and can never be separated from his love.

It's good thing after good thing, undeserved, unmerited, free of charge. Over and over we see the activity of the triune God – Father, Son, Spirit – working for our good. And it's all mercy. It's all grace.

In Romans 9, Paul points to God's sovereignty. He doesn't have to show mercy, but he chooses to have mercy – no one is twisting his arm, he is free and it's just what he is like! The life that he offers isn't only for the Jews, in chapter 10, but for all nations, 'for "Everyone who calls on the name of the Lord will be saved' (Romans 10.13, quoting Joel 2.32). Paul presses this further in chapter 11. Where the nation of Israel had been the focus of his work until now, through Jesus Christ, God has made a way for all nations to be reconciled. And he finishes this section and chapter 11 with this uncontainable burst of praise:

> Oh, the depth of the riches of the wisdom and knowledge
>   of God!
>   How unsearchable his judgments,
>   and his paths beyond tracing out!
> Who has known the mind of the Lord?
>   Or who has been his counsellor?
> Who has ever given to God,
>   that God should repay them?
> For from him and through him and for him are all things.
>   To him be the glory for ever! Amen.
>
> (Romans 11.33–36)

Paul paints an amazing picture: a huge and beautiful panoramic view of God's mercy. It reminds me of going on holiday with my parents to a place in North Wales – it's a beautiful place but there is this one particular point, on a slightly hidden and rarely used cliff path to a beach, where we'd stop to take in the view. We would see a boundless view of sea, sky, beach, sand dunes, forest, mountains in the distance, a castle above the dunes, a golf course and cliffs – massive, beautiful, filling our entire view, stretching to the horizon. The vast and gorgeous landscape of Romans 11 is full of the manifold and expansive mercies of God: 'This mercy, this mercy! He's done this, and this, and this . . .'

After showing how God sent Jesus to die for us – how he has forgiven us, reconciled us, adopted us, called us and chosen us; how he has given us his Spirit and new life, and made us a new creation; how he gives us power to fight sin, invites us to call him Father and to know a love that we can never lose – after all that, Paul says, '*Therefore*, I urge you, brothers and sisters, in view of God's mercy, to offer your bodies as a living sacrifice, holy and pleasing to God – this is your true and proper worship' (Romans 12.1, emphasis added).

Paul pulls together all that he has been saying about the mercies of God as the reason and grounds for what he is about to require from his hearers. It's the motivation, the power, the 'why'. But it leads somewhere; he doesn't stop at reflection, he doesn't stop at wonder, he moves from it to an outflow, to a 'doing'. And it's this: 'be a living sacrifice'.

OFFER YOUR BODIES AS A LIVING SACRIFICE, HOLY AND PLEASING TO GOD (ROMANS 12.13)

But what does that mean? Well, in a nutshell, it means 'surrender'. It means, 'be change in God's pocket'. Paul is drawing on imagery and practice from his own culture; this statement is thick with Old Testament symbolism. The Israelite nation would bring animals to the temple and they would be placed on the altar and killed as a sacrifice, sometimes for sin, sometimes for worship or as part of a festival and so on. Whatever it was for, the animal placed on the altar lost its life (see, for example, Leviticus and Numbers). Paul uses this imagery, something that his readers would all have understood, and throws a couple of curve balls; we are to offer ourselves, not a substitute animal, but our whole lives, and moreover not as dead but alive. We are to be dedicated to the Lord, completely, every part of us, fully surrendered, like a sacrifice but alive.

We find this idea of being dead but alive a number of times in Paul's letters. We are to be dead to sin but alive to Christ (Romans 6.11); we are to die to our old way of life, our old self (Ephesians 4.22–24), and to find new life and new birth in Jesus. Baptism is an illustration of this: death and life, burial and birth (Romans 6.4). Paul's writing communicates the degree of change undergone by the Christian. The person who has experienced the grace of God, who has met and accepted Jesus, hasn't just added him to their lives, as you might a fashion accessory, but has been radically changed. The imagery in Paul is stark: they have gone from darkness to light (Colossians 1.13), from death to life; they are a new creation (1 Corinthians 5.17) or, as he writes to the Galatian Church: 'I have been crucified with Christ and I no longer live, but Christ lives in me. The life I now live in the body, I live by faith in the Son of God, who loved me and gave himself for me' (Galatians 2.20). The language is strong; death and life, dead but alive. In all these strong images, Paul is articulating the central move from living for ourselves towards living for God – being surrendered to his will and desire.

In the Old Testament, the sacrificed animals were deemed to be a 'pleasing aroma' to the Lord (Numbers 15.3), and Paul draws on this; it is our living fully surrendered to him that is to be the pleasing aroma. All this imagery is painting a vivid picture. He is saying to the Church in Rome, 'Be fully surrendered to Jesus, in all your living and doing, so that his purposes are your purposes.' We are to be those who have given up their own agenda to be about Jesus. We are to be alive and completely surrendered to him.

There is so much we could say about this passage but I want to make three quick observations that I think are important to note. First, it's a response. I have already mentioned it but it is so important to see that the first part of the verse is the grounds for the second part. Surrender isn't meant to be something that we try *really* hard to achieve. The key idea in the passage is that of response. I remember John Stott quoting Thomas Erskine of Linlathen, who put it this way: 'The New Testament religion is grace, and ethics is gratitude.'[3] That is exactly the idea here and all through the Bible. Our 'doing' for God has to stem from, be grounded in, be a response to, his 'doing' for us.

Every other religion in the world has a system that is based upon achieving, meriting God's favour, doing something in order to gain something. Christianity is the only religion where everything is a free gift of grace, and our 'doing' is only ever a response to that grace, not a way to merit it. Surrendering, or being a 'living sacrifice', is secondary: it is dependent on seeing God's mercy because it is an action born of gratitude. I once heard someone put it this way: 'Let the imperatives marinate in the indicatives.' They meant the same thing – don't let the gospel calls to 'doing and living' stand alone, first place them deeply and firmly in the things that are true of us and God in the gospel.

Paul is deliberate in keeping it sequential, from God's doing to our doing. Otherwise we will begin to bring in some of the conditional mentality that is our tendency, where we start to feel bad if we aren't doing well, or good if we are. Paul spends time countering this mindset in a number of letters. In his letter to the Galatians, he clearly articulates the need to recognise grace and salvation as free, undeserved, unmerited gifts (see Galatians 1—3), independent of our goodness or badness. Unless it starts with God's doing and then our responding, we will start to see our doing as in some way contributing to, or 'earning', God's action on our behalf! That's not the gospel. The gospel, for Paul, is all about what God has done, what he has given: free, unmerited favour. Surrender is a response to the kindness of God that has already been freely given. It's a response. We are to live *from* God's grace not *for* God's grace.

And it's one of the themes that I wanted to articulate in 'I Am Yours', the language of our giving being primarily in response to him, born of gratitude. One of the key lines in the chorus places statements of what we will do for God squarely as a response to

God. It's almost borrowing language straight from this passage when the song says, 'In light of all you've done for me, I lay my life down at your feet.'

Second, in addition to surrender being a response to God's mercy and kindness, it is actually called worship. The verse ends with 'this is your true and proper worship'. Yes, we sing songs and call that worship, but the heart of worship has to be more than that. This surrendering, this dying to ourselves and living for Christ, this emptying ourselves of our own agenda and being fully available to God's, whatever the cost, this being 'change in God's pocket' – this is true and proper worship. We see this about worship again and again – it must be more than words. When Jesus encounters some Pharisees in Matthew, he quotes the Old Testament and says, 'These people honour me with their lips, but their hearts are far from me. They worship me in vain' (Matthew 15.8–9). Clearly, lip service with absent hearts is not worship. In Amos, we read that when justice and mercy were missing, God says, 'I hate, I despise your religious festivals . . . Away with the noise of your songs! I will not listen to the music of your harps' (Amos 5.21, 23). Clearly, singing without real action or godliness is not worship. True religion in James is that which looks after 'orphans and widows' (James 1.27). Over and over we see that worship isn't only words, but is always more than that. That's not to say that words and songs are not important, just that they are not the whole picture. Here in Romans, Paul clarifies that worship, true and proper worship, is grounded in a surrendered life. It is living our whole lives for him.

Third, in addition to surrender being a response and worship, it's reasonable. That final line is translated in different ways: some equate 'true and proper worship' with 'reasonable service'. I actually quite like that. It suggests that, ultimately, in light of God's extravagant grace and mercy, the offering of our whole lives makes sense. It's reasonable. Anything less would be unreasonable or out of balance. In light of what he has done, giving up the glory of heaven for the squalor of the cross for us, the surrendering of our whole lives to him is nothing more than reasonable service. If what he has done is really true then it makes sense. In Philippians, Paul instructs his hearers to live a life 'worthy of the gospel' (Philippians 1.27). The word 'worthy' here means 'in balance with', 'in continuity with' or 'of equal weight to'. It's a similar idea – if the gospel is true, if God did all that we believe him to have done, then what sort of life would make sense? What sort of living would be reasonable? What would be a logical response? Full surrender. I really wanted to capture this idea, that it's in light of the cross, it's in light of all that he has done that we surrender to him, that we offer ourselves. Given what he gave, giving ourselves is really nothing more than reasonable service.

So, what on earth does all this mean to us today? Do we all have to sell everything and go abroad? Well, for some that is the case. I recently read of Jim Elliot, a young man who went with a number of others to Ecuador to reach a hidden group of people called the Huaorani with the gospel. Despite making some initial progress with them, Jim Elliot and his companions were suddenly killed. The Huaorani had attacked them and their bodies were found down river a few days later. Evangelising cost Jim the ultimate price. Some time later they found Jim's journal, containing his personal reflections. Jim had been reading Jesus' words, 'What will it profit a man if he gains the whole world and forfeits his soul?' (Matthew 16.26 ESV), and he wrote, this profound sentence: 'He is no fool who gives up what he cannot keep, in order to gain what he cannot lose.'[4] What amazing words. What cost! What gain! It echoes Paul's words elsewhere: 'I count everything as loss because of the surpassing worth of knowing Christ Jesus my Lord' (Philippians 3.8 ESV). Everything is laid on the altar. History is littered with stories about Christians who gave up their comforts and embraced the costs – even giving up their lives – for what they believed.

Dietrich Bonhoeffer was one, a Christian scholar in Germany during the Second World War who opposed the Nazi regime. As a result, he was thrown into a concentration camp and was eventually killed for his opposition. But it was an opposition born out of his faith, out of his commitment to Jesus. He famously wrote the line: 'When Christ calls a man, he bids him come and die.'[5] It was his way of saying 'offer your bodies as a living sacrifice', totally surrendered. This is happening around the world today. Recently, I was leading worship at an event run by Open Doors, a charity that works to support the persecuted Church around the world, and I was challenged again by stories of terrible persecution but also incredible courage as Christians hold on to faith and follow Jesus at the greatest cost, surrendering everything. In our context, in my context – that is, Western Christianity – we aren't really confronted with those sorts of situations, with life and death decisions, but the call remains the same – in comfort or in discomfort, in privilege or in persecution, are we about the purposes of God? Are we fully surrendered to him? Are we 'living sacrifices'?

We face decisions every day where we need to surrender again to the purposes of God. We desire things that we know aren't right, we are tempted to do things that we shouldn't, to not do things that we should; we are tempted and allured by the materialism and immediacy of the pleasure-pursuing culture we live in. It's seductive and dangerous. As in the Parable of the Sower, it would be easy to be among those whose seed is choked by the 'cares of the world' (Mark 4.19), or like the Laodicean Church in Revelation, it would be easy to become 'lukewarm' and risk being spat out of God's mouth (see Revelation 3.16). Every day, minute by minute, we face the decision to surrender to Jesus' call, to extend his Kingdom, to be different *or* to conform and be shaped by society.

For me, at the time of writing the song, it had a specific outworking. I recognised an inconsistency between what I believed and what I did. I believed that the gospel was hugely important with eternal significance, the only real hope for the world, and yet I would walk past people all the time without ever trying to talk to them about it. In a general sense, I worked for a church and I was very much 'for' telling people about Jesus, but personally, or when I wasn't 'at work', I didn't really do a huge amount about it. I remember thinking that I wanted to talk to people about Jesus, but it scared me and so at the same time I didn't want to.

One afternoon, I found myself walking past some street preachers and, while thinking that the medium they were using wasn't really working, and being embarrassed by them in many ways, I also found myself feeling challenged and envious. They seemed to have decided that it didn't matter whether they seemed foolish; that nothing would stop their telling people about Jesus. The issue I had was that I wanted people to like me; I didn't want to look silly. However, I increasingly began to feel as if I wasn't change in God's pocket. He couldn't just spend me as he chose: in reality, he could spend me as I chose, or truer still, I could spend me as I chose! And so, one day, a friend and I decided to go out and try to talk to people about Jesus. It was horrible. I did not enjoy it. We swallowed our pride, approached people and said, 'Can I talk to you about Jesus?' I remember even paying a busker for two minutes of his time, so that I could talk to him about Jesus and pray with him! There were a few good conversations but, on the whole, we were a long way from revival; however, I came away feeling the Lord's pleasure. It was a moment of surrender, of saying, 'Not my will but yours.' It threw me into a time of trying to go and talk to people about Jesus, and every time it felt like climbing on to the altar, placing my pride there.

There was one occasion when I went up to this guy to talk to him about Jesus and I could tell he wanted to get away. After not very long, I cut my losses and said, 'Look, could you give me some feedback? How was this for you?' He looked very confused. So I carried on, 'It's just that I want to talk to people about Jesus but I don't know what works and what doesn't. What do you think? What's your experience of this moment?' He clearly believed I had lost it but thought for a moment and then helpfully said, 'Maybe you could do it in the daylight, in public – where there are other people!' And I realised that he had a point: 11 p.m. in the pitch black, with no one else around, wasn't the best time to share the gospel!

I went on this journey where I had to surrender to Jesus, I had to be willing for him to spend me as he pleased. It's not easy.

But God is looking for people who are surrendered, who think less of their ego and more of God's fame; who think less of their own comfort and more about the Kingdom. He is looking for people who recognise that the value of the gospel far outweighs every other concern; who recognise that it is more valuable than any other thing – like the pearl merchant, in Matthew 13, who sells everything he has to gain the pearl of great worth (Matthew 13.45). God is looking for surrendered people, sold out people, 'living sacrifices'. And it doesn't have to be selling everything and going abroad – it's quite likely to involve doing something right where you are. So, how do we do it?

First, we must remember regularly. If 'response' is such a key component in what it means to surrender – that it's 'in light of all that he has done' – then we need to make sure that we don't stray too far from the mercy of God, from recalling it, from experiencing it, from the centrality of the cross. Jerry Bridges writes that we should 'preach the gospel to ourselves daily'. That we should remember that we were sinners in need of a saviour and that God in his great mercy made a way for us to be reconciled to him. We must remember that we have been forgiven; that we are beneficiaries of all his kindnesses; that we are Spirit-filled, adopted children, co-heirs with Christ, inheritors of eternal life, chosen, called – the list goes on and on.

Given the society we live in, the enemy who lies and our own tendency to stray, we simply cannot afford to stop reminding ourselves of this. I grew up in a Christian family; my dad was a pastor and I had been following Jesus from a young age in a pretty committed way. But there was a moment in the summer of my second year at university where the grace and mercy of God hit me in a new, fresh and powerful way. It was a moment of clarity. I remember being at a conference and singing the song 'Here is love vast as the ocean' and sobbing through it as the grace of God touched me deeply, in a way that I hadn't experienced before. I realised I needed to hold on to the clarity of that moment, to remember the importance of God's grace. I knew that it would begin to grow distant in my memory soon, that the immediacy of the sense of his grace on my heart would fade. So, to help me remember, I went a few days later and bought a ring, which I still wear today. It has 'The pearl of great price' inscribed on it, and it acts as a reminder. I don't want to forget! We have to stay near to the mercy of God; we have to remember regularly if we are to keep the fuel of surrendered living topped up.

We have to remember regularly but we also have to surrender regularly. It doesn't seem to be something that we do once and then it's done. It's a way of life and it seems that our tendency is to continually veer away from it. Someone once said that the problem with a 'living sacrifice' is that it keeps climbing off the altar. One of the reasons for that is because surrender involves self-denial. There are things that we would like, would love, that we are required to let go of or lay down. There is a cost to surrender. It's not easy. However, despite the cost, I suspect the gains are far greater than anything we lay down. David Livingstone, the well-known nineteenth-century missionary to Africa, who gave up everything for the gospel, finished by saying, 'I never made a sacrifice.'[6] Of course, on the one hand, he did sacrifice many things but, in his own view – in comparison to the extent of the mercy of God he was responding to, the blessing of God's presence and the sense of God's saying 'Well done, good and faithful servant'. It was as if he had never made a sacrifice: such is the soul satisfaction to be found in surrendering to God. Jesus says a similar thing to the disciples when they say how much they have given up for him – their gain will be 'a hundred times as much' (Matthew 19.29). But in the here and now – with the cost, the self-denial, our transient emotions and desiring hearts – we really need to climb back on the altar and say, 'God, I'm yours, use me as you please,' with a daily, if not hourly, regularity.

One habit that can help is the prayer of indifference.[7] It's an Ignatian prayer. Ignatius was a theologian in seventeenth-century Spain, who spent time thinking about habits and practices that would keep us mindful of God. One of them was practising indifference. The term 'indifference' sounds negative, like maybe 'lazy' or 'indecisive' or 'lacking passion, zeal or care'. But Ignatius doesn't use it in that way. Instead we are to pray, 'God make me indifferent to anything other than your purposes.' Our own agenda, our success or lack of it, our own wants and desires are to become secondary to the purposes of God. And so we pray, 'God make me indifferent to anything but your will and purpose, indifferent to anything that doesn't cause me to love you more.' That is a prayer of surrender; it's a prayer for 'climbing back on the altar'. We need to surrender regularly.

God has called us to be surrendered people but it's a surrender that is born from our knowing and experiencing his radical love for us. We go anywhere because he went anywhere; we do anything because he did everything. All *our* 'doing' is grounded in, motivated by, in light of, *his* doing. Surrender is the response of grateful hearts; it is the response of people who have understood grace. And so the one thing we must always do is stay clinging to the cross. Paul, in his letter to the Corinthians, when faced with the temptation to show strength to get their favour, instead decided not to. He writes, 'For I resolved to know nothing while I was with you except Jesus Christ and him crucified' (1 Corinthians 2.2). I love that language. Never stray from the cross, never graduate from being a recipient of undeserved mercy, never grow out of the sense of gratitude you had at first, never allow your love to grow cold or your heart to become hard. Stay close to the cross, mindful of his mercies; live from there because that's where the power, the reason, the fuel for surrender is found.

The Kingdom, the gospel, is a cause to live for; it's a cause to die for, to do anything or go anywhere for; and it advances through the lives of willing people. Surrendered people are the sort of people that God is seeking and the sort of people that the world is needing. It is God's desire *for us*, it's what the world needs *from us*, it's the calling *on us*, so let's sing and pray that it would be true *of us*.

What God couldn't do with a generation of individuals who, in response to his grace and mercy, cry out, 'All I have I'm laying down before you. Here I am, use me for your glory.' What if we were that generation, a living sacrifice, sold out, change in his pocket, fully surrendered, indifferent to anything else? I think we would see the world change, and I wouldn't be at all surprised if, in giving everything we had, we found Livingstone's words on our own lips: 'I never made a sacrifice.'

NOTES

1. <http://www.vineyardchurches.org.uk/about/john-wimber/> (accessed 9 August 2018).
2. <https://www.mljtrust.org/free-sermons/book-of-romans/3/> (accessed 9 August 2018). The turning point, six minutes in.
3. <https://us.langham.org/bible_studies/2-june-2016/> (accessed 9 August 2018).
4. <https://www.brainyquote.com/quotes/jim_elliot_189244>.
5. Dietrich Bonhoeffer, *The Cost of Discipleship* (New York: Touchstone, 1995). First published in German as *Nachfolge* (Munich: Christian Kaiser Verlag, 1937).
6. <https://www.desiringgod.org/articles/i-never-made-a-sacrifice> (accessed 9 August 2018).
7. <https://www.ignatianspirituality.com/27475/ignatian-indifference> (accessed 9 August 2018).

Notes

VINEYARD VALUES

In the late 80s the first Vineyard churches in Europe were started in the UK. Fast forward thirty years and those churches have multiplied repeatedly across the United Kingdom and Ireland. Small groups of people have become a movement of tens of thousands of people in over one hundred and thirty locations.

The values that were present in those first churches continue to run through the DNA of every Vineyard church. This book takes some of these key values and unpacks them for a new generation, with voices from around our global family contributing to each chapter.

This book also contains a Leader's Guide to help run an 'Introduction to the Vineyard' Small Group, ideal for sharing our history, values and vision to Extend God's Kingdom Together Everywhere in Every Way.

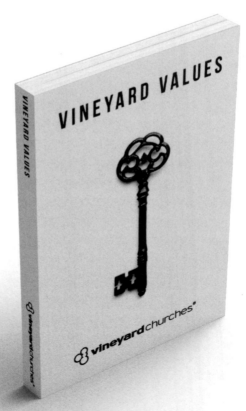